First published in 1999 by
Mercier Press
5 French Church Street Cork
Tel: (021) 275040; Fax (021) 274969
E-mail: books@mercier.ie
16 Hume Street Dublin 2
Tel: (01) 661 5299; Fax: (01) 661 8583
E-mail: books@marino.ie

Trade enquiries to CMD Distribution
55A Spruce Avenue
Stillorgan Industrial Park
Blackrock County Dublin
Tel: (01) 294 2556; Fax: (01) 294 2564

© Tony Flannery 1999

ISBN 1 85635 244 7

10 9 8 7 6
A CIP record for this title is available
from the British Library

Cover design by Penhouse Design
Printed in Ireland by ColourBooks,
Baldoyle Industrial Estate, Dublin 13

FROM THE INSIDE

FROM THE INSIDE

A PRIEST'S VIEW
OF THE CATHOLIC CHURCH

TONY FLANNERY

MERCIER PRESS

Contents

INTRODUCTION

One of the commonly used phrases to describe the Church in Catholicism is to say that it is our mother. I have been a servant of the Church since my early teens. I have spent thirty-five years in religious life and twenty-five as a priest. 'Mother' is not the word that would come easily to mind if I was asked to describe the Church as I have known it. Certainly not the idealised image that word normally tends to convey in this context. The Church gave me a kind but narrow and puritanical education. Like most Catholics of my generation, it imbued me with a lot of guilt, especially about sexuality and my body. At various times throughout my life in the Church I have known it to be authoritarian, dogmatic, devious, self-serving and even on occasion corrupt. But it has also opened up for me a world of great depth and beauty; it has been a gateway to mystery and to the realm of the spirit. I have experienced kindness, support and encouragement. For me it has had many faces, good and bad. Maybe in that way it is similar to what a real human mother is like, so 'Mother' might not be a bad name for it after all.

From my experience of other priests I am not sure how typical I am of priests in general. I certainly never had any 'road-to-Damascus' experience to convince me that I had this thing called a 'vocation'. Experts in the modern understanding of the human person and in human motivation, would probably say that I ended up as a priest through the excessively strong influence of family, school and general environment. Being the youngest of a family of four, all of whom had entered religious life before me, and having gone at the age of twelve to a junior seminary, whose purpose was to shape young men into suitable candidates for priesthood and which was strong on mind control, I can see now that I was definitely steered in that direction. So it is hard to assess how free my choice was at the different stages along the way.

Not that any of that matters now. People make life decisions for all sorts of complex reasons, conscious and unconscious. I have never been very convinced of this notion of a special call to the priesthood which is different and more special than the choices the rest of humanity make in their lives. Despite the fact that I have had a busy and very satisfying twenty-five years working as a priest, I do know that I have never made the sort of commitment that a lot of the priests of my generation seem to have made. By that I mean that I have never shut out the possibility of changing direction in my life. I don't ever quite remember taking the phrase 'You are a priest forever' as final. There was always for me the possibility that I might do something else next year. And there still is. Maybe that is the reason why I have tended from a very early stage to see myself as being a little on the fringe of the Church, observing it in a somewhat more dispassionate way than the average priest. But don't get me wrong. I am not looking for sympathy. I have had, and continue to have, a good life. Whenever I am asked if I would do it over again if I had another chance, I answer no, definitely not. But that is not casting aspersions on the life

I have had. It is rather a recognition of the immense variety of experience available to the human person and of how little can be lived in one lifetime. So if I had another life, and I would love to get another go at it (I can see why people are attracted to belief in reincarnation), there would be so many other experiences I would wish to savour. If they were as fulfilling as this life has been, that would be fine.

So for now I remain a priest, and a busy one. I have worked through twenty-five dramatic, exciting and, more recently, traumatic years in the Irish Church. In this book, which is part biography and part the story of the Church from the inside during those years, I have tried to tell it as I have experienced it. I have attempted to write with a minimum of theology, and even less religiosity, so that the narrative will be easily accessible to the average reader who lived through those years with me and who was inevitably affected to a greater or lesser extent by the events about which I write. I have tried to tell it as truthfully as I possibly can. Surprisingly, that does not come too easily to a priest. We are so deeply embedded in the system, so much servants of the Church, that there is a powerful tendency in us to paint our lives and our work with a rosier colour than they deserve, so that we will not bring any opprobrium on the institution. I have tried to avoid this. Many of the events that I write about, like the social debates, the contraception issue, and the clerical scandals, were major items of news in this country. Other people may have very different versions of these same events. That is fine. I simply write about them from my own particular perspective and experience. In describing and attempting to analyse the type of training my generation of priests received in religion and sexuality, I am attempting to help the ordinary person to understand why some of the present problems are besetting the Church, and why we priests often tend to adopt attitudes that appear incomprehensible to those outside the clerical state.

As you, the reader, will no doubt quickly observe, in writing this book I am also doing what I presume most people who attempt some form of biographical writing are doing; I am coming to terms with, and even purging aspects of, my own past. I hope that in reading it you will gain something of the value that the writing has been for me.

1

A Priest for Ever – Maybe

I was ordained a priest in June of 1974 by Bishop Tom Ryan of Clonfert. This was the man who, because of one injudicious phone call made in response to an item on the *Late Late Show*, became forever associated in the public mind with a nightie. In reality he was a nice, ordinary type of man. The worst thing that ever happened to him was that he was made a bishop. He was lonely in that big house outside Loughrea, and for a man who was sociable by nature and who needed human company at an ordinary level, to be a bishop (with his understanding of what that role involved) meant that he was cut off and isolated from the very thing he most needed.

That evening I returned home to my own village where I got a royal welcome. Bonfires were lit, the village was bedecked with bunting, a platform was erected outside my parents' house and everybody gathered. Speeches were made by various neighbours. My father thanked them all for their welcome and when I spoke they listened with great silence and respect. The following day I said my first Mass in the local church and after that it was open house, open turf shed (equipped with a temporary timber floor for dancing) and open hay shed (with a keg of Guinness and a keg of lager from which my uncle doled liberal measures) for the rest of the day. Everybody queued up for my first blessing and handed me a fairly generous donation. That was all lovely; when it comes to a community celebrating some event, the Irish rural parish has little to learn.

But I also became aware that in some serious way things had changed. I began to receive deference from people who I thought had no reason whatsoever to defer to me. Men and women twice my age, friends of my parents, who in themselves had achieved considerable wisdom and experience of life and whom I had often heard expounding wisely on things now began to address me as 'Father' and, worse still, agree with everything I was saying. I began to hear for the first time that response I have come to hate: 'Yes, Father,' or 'That's right, Father'. I must have known that this was part of the life of a priest but it did not hit home until it began to happen to myself. I was now set apart. The faith of these people told them that I was special, that because of what had taken place that morning I was now in some way more holy than they were, that I had great and mysterious powers, that I had blessed hands. A mixture of faith and superstition told them that I had power to do many wonderful things, to bring healing, to impose and to lift curses, to choose whom to bless and whom not to bless, even, on occasions, to tell the future. And along with all of this there was the ordinary functions of the priest in terms of administering the sacraments and celebrating the Eucharist. The country folklore about the power of the priest was endless. Some of it dated back as far as the priests and priestesses of the old pagan religions. But maybe the most dangerous of all, from the young priest's point of view, was the belief that I had suddenly achieved special wisdom and that my opinions were now of considerably more importance than before. Was there an element of fear in this deference? Did they consider it better to keep this person with these strange powers on their side?

I know that this is not the full picture. There was another side to the Irish character that took a much less serious view of the priest. Some people had great ability to stand back and laugh at the posturing of the clergy and to ridicule the pomposity and self-importance of the Church. But still we priests were set apart. While all the time I felt the same as I had the previous day, for me nothing had changed, except that I had achieved my goal and was now ready to begin the active and fruitful part of my life. I was excited about that but I wanted to remain *me*. I did not want to assume any role that would make me different. At least that is what I told myself. But having a position of status, being looked up to and having power over people, are tempting powers for a young man to have. It could easily go to the head, and I know that it did go to mine, at least for a period of time.

I recently listened to a young priest, two years ordained, lecturing his parishioners on the evils of *Fair City*, of all things. I was amused by his utter conviction about his rightness, his belief in his authority over these people and that he could tell them what to think, even about something as ordinary as a television programme, and that he did not consider either his lack of age or experience to be a hindrance. The fact that he was a priest was all the authority he needed. I could see so much of myself in my early years in the way he spoke. He had begun to believe that ordination had conferred on him not just the power to do the priestly things, but also extra wisdom and knowledge, which put him above these people in front of him. He had become arrogant. It was not totally his own fault. Generations of deference by the people to him and his predecessors in the clergy, of acceptance of the priest's power over them, of belief that the priest knew best what was good for the people, had contributed to making priests into what they too often became: men who exercised power over their people, rather than being what they were ordained to be, the servants of the people. I too was to develop my own brand of arrogance but that was later. At first what I was burdened down by was my sense of inadequacy for the task ahead.

I have a strongly accented voice. During my seminary years this had been brought home to me, and I was made aware that it could constitute a serious problem. Twice I was sent to a speech therapist, to see if she could do anything for me. Before I entered the seminary nobody had ever told me there was anything wrong with it. In primary school I tended to be chosen to do readings. So it was an unpleasant revelation to be informed that I had an excessively husky voice and that I could not pronounce my 'r's properly. I pronounced them in a guttural fashion, like the French. And where an 'r' was followed by a broad vowel, such as in the word 'road', it tended to get lost in my throat entirely. My teacher in the seminary was part of the traditional school of elocution, which taught that there was only one correct way to pronounce the English language, and that was the Oxford way.

Anyway I think it is generally true that there is little a speech therapist can do to change a twenty-year-old's basic pronunciation. By then habit has become much too deeply ingrained. She tried hard, and for months I was going around attempting to pronounce 'r's with my tongue flat at the back of my throat, and arched in front behind the upper front teeth. It was a futile exercise and eventually she and I gave up. Years later the same elocution teacher tried again, sending me to a different therapist. He had warned me that unless I managed to conquer this defect I would have to spend my life writing sermons containing no word with the letter 'r'. This therapist, however, was a sensible woman, who quickly recognised the futility of what she was being asked to do. She belonged to the new era that favoured regional accents, as long as they were distinct. She told me I was fine, and sent me home. But inevitably all of this had created a fairly major complex in me as regards my voice, which I carried into ordination. And I was ordained into an institute that specialised in preaching. If I did not measure up in this area, I would be a failure.

After the ordination celebrations were over I went for a few weeks to work in a parish in Coventry. It was my first outing as a priest. I was among total strangers in a foreign country. I was going to find out whether or not I had a problem with my voice. My first Sunday passed off without incident. I was immensely relieved that nobody either walked out or began to laugh when I spoke. They even seemed to be listening. At the end of my few weeks, on the last Sunday, when the final Mass was over and I had said my farewell to the people and they had gone home, I noticed that one old woman remained at the back of the church. Seeing me come out onto the sanctuary she got up and with the help of a walking stick began to come towards me. I went down to meet her. She shook my hand and said: 'Thank you for your sermons. You have a lot of talent. Don't waste it.'

That was all she said but it was what I wanted to hear. I suspect now that she knew that; she had sensed my insecurity and my need for some encouragement. Whatever her reasons for saying what she did, I felt ten feet tall. Somebody had listened to me and thought that I was good. I could do it. I wasn't going to be a misfit or a joke. I might even become a good preacher. My complexes fell away and I returned from Coventry with much more confidence in myself. It is amazing how something so simple, happening at such a crucial moment in your life, can make such a difference. I have since learned that having an unusual sounding voice, as long as it is clear and distinct and not grating, is a positive advantage in public speaking.

I am a member of the Redemptorist congregation. Our specialist work is the preaching of missions, retreats and novenas. So we are in a sense itinerant preachers. It is fairly high pressure work, in the sense that, somewhat like the theatre, you need a full house in order to have a really good mission. With half the church empty there is a lack of atmosphere and excitement about the event. One of the first missions I gave, in a large town in the west of Ireland, was a bit of a disaster. It had more to do with poor planning and organisation than with any lack of interest of the people. The first night went badly, with one of the older men giving a very traditional sermon. I was due to preach the next night. It was a big church, which could seat over a thousand people. When the time came to start there were little more than a hundred people present, almost all elderly.

It was one of the hardest talks I ever had to give in my

life. There was no atmosphere or life in the church and I was depressed and downcast by the poor attendance. I hadn't yet developed the ability to see the people rather than the empty spaces and anyway I knew that what I had to say was not geared towards the age group that were gathered to listen to me. Missions thrive on creating the impression that everyone is there, and that if you don't come you will be missing something. That is why they can still be very successful in places that have a strong community spirit. Their purpose is to renew and revitalise the faith of a community. They are in the same tradition as the Evangelical revivalist meetings. They have a long history in this country, going back into the early part of the last century, and they have built up their own fund of stories and folklore.

Patrick Kavanagh gives a description of the Wednesday night of the mission (traditionally the night that dealt with sex) in his book *Tarry Flynn*. He says that the sermon was so graphic that it gave the men of the parish ideas they never had before. 'Men who had forgotten what they were born for came out . . . ready to bull cows,' while Tarry's mother, wanting to see her son settle down, hoped, 'that the Missioners' condemnation of sex would have the effect of drawing attention to it.'

He also brings out well the strong social and religious pressure there was on people to attend the mission.

'You'll have to go to this Mission every evening, Tarry. I don't want to have the people talking, and its talking they'd be. The last time there was a Mission in this parish . . . the devil a go the Carlins ever went and their luck wasn't much the better of it.'

So, if you didn't attend the mission, the neighbours would

talk about you, and you wouldn't have any luck.

James Joyce, in *A Portrait of the Artist as a Young Man*, though he does it in the context of a school retreat, gives a flavour, albeit something of an upmarket one, of the traditional mission sermon on Hell.

> O, what a dreadful punishment! An eternity of endless agony, of endless bodily and spiritual torment, without one ray of hope, without one moment of cessation, of agony limitless in intensity, of torment infinitely varied, of torture that sustains eternally that which it eternally devours, of anguish that everlastingly preys upon the spirit while it racks the flesh, an eternity, every instant of which is itself an eternity of woe. Such is the terrible punishment decreed for those who die in mortal sin by an almighty and a just God.

My ancestors in the Redemptorists are generally known as 'hellfire' preachers, because of the graphic way they preached about hell, though by the time I came along most of that had disappeared. I think the reputation tended to be built around a few individuals, who were both colourful and extreme in their style of preaching. The average Redemptorist missioner of the past was a more gentle figure than the folklore suggests. When I asked one man, now dead, if he preached on hell, he told me that he did, because it was one of the prescribed subjects of the time, but he commented: 'In my sermons the fires of hell were fuelled by very wet turf!'

Sigerson Clifford, the Kerry poet, brings out some of the gentleness of the traditional mission in his poem about the coming of the missioners to a small rural parish during the winter:

> The night-time was the worst of all
> The hours dragged slow and lame.
> The great diversion that we had
> Was when the missioners came.
> We were only middling sinners
> With little venials to our score.
> So they blessed our beads and left us
> And the night flowed back once more.

The work of a preacher of parish missions is now much more difficult and challenging than it was when I began twenty-five years ago. When you invite people to come to the church for forty-five minutes to an hour each evening for a week, which is what we do on a mission, you are now competing with an enormous range of other activities and interests. It is a different world from the time of Sigerson Clifford, when the mission was the only diversion. Now you compete with *Coronation Street* four nights of the week and in all probability Manchester United, Liverpool or the Irish soccer team will be playing live on television on one of the nights. Generally people's lives are much more active and busy than they used to be. The old sense of obligation about attending religious ceremonies that Kavanagh talks about is largely gone, even in the countryside. Schooled by the modern media, people's expectations are much higher than they used to be in terms of the quality of communication and the general presentation they look for. If they come one night and are either bored or turned off by what is presented to them, they will not return. So it is increasingly becoming specialist work. Yet when I began in the early seventies, despite the odd flop, most missions were automatically well attended.

I must have been only about a year at the work when I found myself, with another priest, in the town of Ballinrobe in County Mayo. My fellow missioner was only a few years older than myself. This was not typical of the traditional mission, which usually had an older man in charge, accompanied by someone younger. Religious life had worked on the basis of seniority, just as the diocesan priesthood still largely operates today. Promotion came with age and the older man was always the superior. A few years previously a revolution had taken place in my religious congregation which had given the power over to the young generation. We were doing missions in a new way, with a new message, and we were full of excitement and energy, with great hope for the future.

It was during the later years of the Papacy of Paul VI, and while he himself had become old and seemed to be a bit disillusioned, the ferment of debate which had been opened up by the Vatican Council was still alive, even if *Humanae Vitae* had put something of a damper on it. And yet, in the Irish Church, there was still a strong sense of stability. True, the liturgical changes had come in and had generally been accepted, without the kind of traditionalist reaction that had happened in Britain. The penny catechism had disappeared, and it took time for an adequate replacement to be developed, so that a generation was growing up who were not getting a grounding in the basics of the faith. The abolition of some of the regulations that had traditionally been imposed under the pain of mortal sin was causing considerable confusion. Despite all this, the Church and the clergy were held in very high esteem. And the large majority of people were still going regularly to Mass, and to missions.

We missioners, even though we believed ourselves to be new types of preachers with a new message, were being carried on the shoulders of the tradition created by our predecessors more than we realised or would care to admit. In this parish we were still continuing one significant aspect of the 'old style' mission, in that we kept the women and the men separated, with a different week for each. It is hard to imagine doing that now but it was common practice in those days. I'm sure it had its origins in the traditional segregation of the sexes but it also had a practical side to it. Women appeared to be more religious by nature and more easily won over. So the logic was to hold their week first and rely upon them to encourage the men to attend. It was working very well, and on the final week the church was packed with men each evening. I was still young enough to be a smoker and once while my fellow missioner was preaching the 'great sermon', which I knew would last for up to half an hour, I decided that I would have time to nip out and have a quiet smoke.

The pocket of my jacket only yielded up an empty cigarette box. I quickly jumped into the car and drove down the little town. It was almost deserted, with the men at the mission and the women at home. There were a number of small shops open but I did not want to walk in unannounced in case there might be a man behind the counter and both he and I would be embarrassed at the fact that the missioner had caught him not attending his mission. So I kept going until I came to a shop were I could see through the window an old woman behind the counter. She welcomed me and told me how lovely the previous week had been. She hoped we were getting on well with the men and that we were 'giving them hell!' She refused to take any payment for the cigarettes. That type of thing was also common in those days. It had a lovely side to it and was partly a reflection of the faith of the people. But it was dangerous for the young priest. Again he was being treated as special and he could easily begin to see it as part of his due and take it for granted.

I suppose in some ways these were the in-between years in Ireland. The Pope's visit had not yet happened. Parts of the country were still very traditional and other parts had begun to move away from the Church. We, the younger missioners and priests, saw ourselves as a new generation, more open and free in ourselves that those who had gone before us, and relating to people in a more informal manner. And in some ways we were. But we were much more products of our tradition and retained much more of both its good and its bad elements than we realised. I was soon to get a salutary and fairly painful lesson in that.

Roscommon is a small town. At least it was twenty years ago; a country town, with little or no element of the cosmopolitan about it. Not too long after the mission I described above, we found ourselves there, this time five of us, to visit the homes of the parish and do something special for the youth, along with the standard week each for the women and the men. It was the month of May, and beautiful in the way that only May can be. After a long hard winter the warmth of the sun felt like new life. The evenings especially were precious, bright and long and calling a person outdoors. Walkers, gardeners, golfers were indulging their particular passion with energy, happy in the thought of the long summer ahead. For the farmers, even the long days of early summer were not sufficient for all that had to be done, with crops to be sown and the first cut of the silage needing attention. Calling people to church for an hour every evening of the week was asking a lot of them. The women, as was their wont, responded well and the church was packed every night. We the missioners, used to that type of response, were not surprised and while we revelled in the excitement of the large crowd, we regarded it as no more than our due. So when the men's week produced only a sparse attendance of old men scattered around the benches, we were downcast.

On the Sunday morning at the beginning of the men's week it was my job to preach at all the Masses. This was an important talk, designed to encourage and entice the men to attend the mission. I had by now been about two years at the work and they had been successful and exciting years for me. Having completely overcome any complex I had about my voice, and no longer worrying about words with the letter 'r' in them, I had discovered that I had a natural gift for public speaking and that my voice had an attractive quality about it that made people sit up and listen. But having a gift for public speaking is a dangerous thing, as history clearly illustrates. I had come to know what it is like to hold a large crowd in the palm of your hand, in a sense to play with their emotions. It is a powerful experience and it brings with it a very deep sense of excitement and satisfaction: the silence in a church, the rapt attention of people as they wait for your next word. The feeling is wonderful. I have never taken illegal drugs but when I hear people talk about their effects and using the word 'high', that is what I associate with it. It is ultimately an experience of power and control, and it is a drug. Public admiration and even adulation were common enough in missions in those days. 'Father, you are a wonderful preacher'; 'I would stand in the snow listening to you'. Unfortunately but almost inevitably, I had come to love this type of adulation and to need it more than I would have admitted or even been aware.

At the biggest Mass on that Sunday morning I was in full flight from the altar delivering my sermon. I spoke without notes, with a roving microphone in my hand as I walked around the perimeter of the altar addressing the people. I had a sense that I was doing well; my adrenalin was flowing, as I strongly encouraged the men of the parish to attend their mission. Why would they not attend! We were definitely the best show in town, and wouldn't it be a chance to hear me preaching! Suddenly I saw a group of men clearly having a chat down in the back porch of the church. Not only were they not in rapt attention, they weren't listening at all. How could they possibly be talking during my sermon! Since I was this 'wonderful preacher', what sort of morons were they not to listen to me? And had they no respect? That was it. Even if they did not find what I was saying interesting, they should have more respect for me and for the Church than to talk while I was preaching. What could I do? Would I say something over the microphone? My train of thought was interrupted and I could sense my uneasiness communicating itself to the people. It is impossible to retain your communication with an audience if your mind is distracted by something else.

'Would the men in the back porch please stop talking!'

Since they had not been listening to me in the first place, they didn't hear my admonition and happily continued their chat. But now the whole church was on edge. I was unable to get my own focus back to them but continued to try, while ostensibly talking to the people in the church in front of me, to win the attention of the men in the porch. I failed and in a state of high emotion and deep feeling I brought my sermon to an end as best I could.

Since I wasn't saying the Mass I returned immediately to the sacristy. I was angry and frustrated, and far too full of uncontrolled emotion to be able to stand back a little and recognise what was going on in me. I felt like going straight down to the back of the church and confronting the men in the porch. I at least had the good sense to consult with one of the older missioners who was sitting in the sacristy. But in this case age did not produce wisdom, and I was advised that if that was the way I felt to go and do it. I walked around the side of the church on the outside and into the porch, where the group of men had now broken off their conversation and fallen silent, as the Mass was nearing the consecration.

They clearly had their own scale of priority, in which the sermon was not important, but the Eucharist still retained its mystery and its significance. For a moment all my illusions about being the new-style priest – down off the pedestal, one of the people, here to serve as an equal – fell away and I became again what some of my precursors in the order had been, as I berated those men for daring to speak while I was preaching. They, being the traditional Irishmen of the time, looked at the ground and remained silent. Having said my say I returned slowly to the sacristy and as my anger cooled I gradually became aware of a very uncomfortable feeling deep inside myself. I began to realise that this had not been my most glorious hour. It is bad enough to have made a fool of yourself, but to have done so in public! Like most people when confronted by an unpalatable fact about themselves, I tried to dismiss it from my mind, telling myself that I had every right to do what I did.

When a mission goes well, with large crowds attending and creating a good atmosphere, and with general enthusiasm and enjoyment of the experience, it can be a very busy week for the missioners but it passes quickly. We draw energy from the people and are carried along by the excitement, and we don't even feel particularly tired until it is over. But a mission week that is badly attended is a very long week for the missioners. There is much less work, so more time to fill. The church is devoid of atmosphere because of the small crowd and there is no buzz around the town about the event. People pass you on the street without even recognising you. The local priests, with whom you are living, are not happy either. They have taken a risk in inviting the missioners and now they realise that they have miscalculated; they will have to pick up the pieces when it is over. With small crowds the collections are poor and how will they pay for the mission?

That week in Roscommon I did not have a lot of demand for my services and I had plenty of time to think, even to brood. I had not yet learned the lesson that crowds aren't everything, and in my eyes the fact that the crowd was small meant that the week was a failure. I increasingly began to accept that this failure had been brought about by the way I had mishandled the previous Sunday. I even imagined, as the week went on, that I began to feel a chill around the town. I had become used to being liked and greatly admired by many people in the parishes where I worked. And while I laughed at these types of responses and genuinely believed they did not affect me, it was still nice to have people feel this way about me. It gave me a sense of importance, a sense that I was special, and might yet do great things. Rejection was a different experience entirely. How does one deal with it? The easiest way is to find someone to blame. And this is how I tried to cope. I found myself saying that this is a tough parish, that the men in this parish are not like elsewhere, that they do not have the faith. My hurt feelings had found a focus and turned into anger and condemnation.

At another level I knew that none of this was true. Another voice was telling me that maybe the men of the parish had made the right decision. Maybe it was better, in the month of May, in the first warmth of the summer sun, to spend your evenings communing with nature than sitting in a church listening to long sermons. Maybe God was more to be found in the hedgerows and the evening breeze. But if that was the case where did it all leave me, the preacher? I was much too insecure to begin to think like that without its taking a big toll of me. When you need to be needed you cannot afford to give people the freedom to take you or leave you as they choose. Looking back now, it is no surprise that the end of that week saw me in the local hospital suffering from severe panic attacks.

Recurring panic attacks, which are a fairly common complaint in the stress-filled world of today, are a very unpleasant type of sickness, as those who have experienced them will know. Their accompanying symptoms - heart palpitations, claustrophobia, depression - are very frightening at first. The first time you suffer from palpitations is a dreadful experience. Your heart begins to beat uncontrollably, pounding inside your chest and seeming as if it is going to jump out. You hear the blood pumping in your ears and you feel that you cannot breathe. It happened to me after dinner one day about half-way through the week, as I was lying in my bed trying to rest and relax. I thought my end had come. The long-term effect of panic attacks is that they undermine your confidence and leave you nervous and unsure. So, from being the apparently cocky, self-confident preacher it now became a struggle for me to face people at all. And getting up in public and preaching a sermon was, for a period of time, a torture.

It isn't often we get a fine summer in Ireland but I spent that one in the late seventies in a state of deep depression. I remember having absolutely no taste for living, lying in bed on beautiful summer days and not wanting to get up. Yet those months, and indeed the next few years, were a time when I learned a very important lesson. What I needed was to get a life for myself independent of my role as the priest or the preacher and out of which I could draw some security and stability. If my security as a person depended on my being a successful and popular priest and missioner, I realised that I would be on very shaky ground in the world into which I was facing. If I built my life totally around my priesthood and my preaching, I would run the considerable risk of doing it all to meet my own needs, as I was doing that Sunday morning in Roscommon, rather than the needs of the people for whom I worked. It is something I have come to recognise as one of the greatest traps in the life of a priest – identifying totally with his role and drawing his personal security from it. This almost inevitably develops into a compulsive need to be liked and popular with his people. Priests who feel this way are often the most hard-working and apparently dedicated but their personal lives can be in turmoil because they are built on such shaky foundations. The work becomes their greatest source of security. They need the people more than the people need them.

My training had taught me that the answers to the problems in life would be found in prayer. It even, as it was so adept at doing, had put a negative twist to the same message by suggesting that the very existence of problems was an indication that not enough prayer was happening in the first place. It had told me that God would sort out the difficulties that a priest might encounter in his life and that He would fill the emptiness of the human heart. So, after the initial debilitating depression, which lasted a few months in my case, I took to prayer with renewed energy and under the guidance of one of the senior members of the community.

It was undoubtedly a help and I don't intend to go into the long and varied story of my spiritual journey since then. But I have come to learn that growth in spirituality and prayer is not a simple matter. There are many pitfalls, sideroads and blind alleys, and the danger of becoming self-absorbed in an unhealthy fashion or even quite self-centred, is very great. I have found it to be true in life that apparent spirituality, in the form of many hours spent in prayer and a great facility at praying, does not always go hand in hand with generosity of spirit, openness and flexibility of attitude, or a willingness to work hard.

The crux lies in the nature of the God we believe in, and

my notion of God has changed many times in the course of my life. I have no belief in the 'God of the gaps', as He is called, or God the miracle-worker. That is the God who when we have a problem in life, must be placated with prayer so that He will sort the problem out. I know that there is some biblical basis for this type of God but I no longer believe in Him. My God is a caring presence, who doesn't need any type of placating or cajoling. Problems in life are precisely that: problems that have to be dealt with at the human level. God's supporting, loving presence will help us through but He will not provide a shortcut through the human struggle of solving the problem.

So if my panic attacks and depression were brought about by unhealthy attitudes and an unhealthy lifestyle, I could pray till my knees were worn away but the problem would not have been solved until I made the necessary adjustments in my life. My God would support and encourage me in that effort. Equally I have no interest in the type of God who offers salvation only to a certain elite group of particularly 'good-living' people, the sort of God that is promoted by many of the fundamentalist sects today and who was a feature of the Catholicism of my youth. The type of spirituality that focuses on getting myself to Heaven is repulsive to me. I have no interest in a salvation that does not encompass humanity. I don't want to live in a paradise from which the bulk of the human race is excluded.

At this point in my life I was lucky. I made new friends, and through them rediscovered the value of physical exercise and a healthy lifestyle. I had played numerous sports with great enthusiasm all through my youth and student days but had stopped taking any form of exercise as soon as I was let loose to work as a priest. A few hours sitting in a tiny cramped confession box, while it may be doing something for the spiritual welfare of the penitents, was certainly of no help to the physical well-being of the priest. Two years of this and I was substantially overweight, unfit, smoking heavily, and beginning to show signs that I could come to depend on alcohol as a way of easing the tensions of life.

Most of us know when our lifestyle is unhealthy and what we should do about it. Getting the motivation to do it is the difficult part. I believe I would not have succeeded on my own. But change was easier now that I had people around me who enjoyed outdoor activities. Through their support I slowly began to adapt. And even at times, especially during the early stages when I was still suffering the effects of the depression, I found myself drawing a good deal of my motivation from my friends. I know this is not the best form of motivation, but when your own self-image has taken a battering, it is as good a way as any of getting over the hump.

Gradually over the next year or two I got my life back into shape. I came to realise the aid that a good walk can be to mental as well as physical health, to appreciate the sense of freedom and relaxation that comes from a swim in the sea, to understand what a great thing it is to spend a day climbing in the hills and to accept that time spent playing a game of golf is not time wasted.

Within a year I had recovered my appetite for the work and I have spent the last twenty-five years working on the mission apostolate around Ireland. By any standards they have been dramatic years and my fellow missioners and myself have been privileged in getting a close-up view of both a church and a society going through extraordinary changes. Because of the nature of our work as missioners we get to travel around the parishes, to live with the priests and come to know the people at a fairly deep level.

I have never been in favour of the traditional black suit. As part of the new image that I wanted to project I, like many other young priests at the time, favoured the wearing of jackets or anoraks. Once, accompanied by another priest, I was conducting the annual retreat in one of the big army barracks. This type of work was never a favourite with me because army retreats tend to be very regimented. I don't know if it is still the case but in those days the soldiers marched in order up to the door of the church. In theory they could fall out at that point and not go in. But in practice it would have been difficult. The officers took up their positions in the front and the ordinary soldiers filled in behind. In this retreat we were trying to break out of the mould and along with the formal retreat sessions we also had group discussions with the men. Hence the presence of two of us, rather than the traditional single preacher. I wore an anorak of a style popular at the time, with a diamond-shaped design, and I must admit it was a fairly shabby garment.

On the final day of the retreat, after the concluding Mass celebrated by the bishop, there was a formal meal with the officers. This took me by surprise, because I hadn't known that it would be part of the schedule. I was at the top table, in between the OC and the next in command. I can still remember the feeling I had when I first observed this scene as I walked into the room. How immaculately dressed all the army men were! I knew that an anorak was not the appropriate garment to be wearing at this function and was making a very different and less complimentary statement on this occasion to the one I wished it to make. During dinner the OC, who was a very cultured gentleman, said to me with some sadness in his voice:

'Since the foundation of the state there have been two great bastions of discipline and control in Irish society. Now, unfortunately, one of them has sold out!'

It said a lot about the way the Church had been perceived in Ireland and about the struggle that was going on at the time. I was fairly clear where I stood. I did not want to be part of an institution that controlled people's lives. That is one of the reasons why I have never worn, and don't even own, a black suit. True, when I am working in the church on a mission I wear my Redemptorist habit which is black – and of course I have long ago discarded the anorak. The black suit is too redolent of the old control and domination exercised by the clergy for me to feel comfortable in it. People have sometimes argued with me that I should wear it for the witness value of it, to proclaim the presence and meaning of the priest. But it is precisely because of the witness factor, that the black suit is for me too much of a witness to the negative sides of clericalism and the Church, that I do not wear it.

The foregoing has been something of my early experiences as a priest in Ireland in the seventies. They were 'the best of times and the worst of times', great years and also very unsettling ones. I have since lived to see dramatic changes in the attitude of the people to the priest. Now we have lost a great deal of the respect and reverence of those times. Instead, the last few years have seen much anger and resentment against the clergy and we are often pilloried and derided. There have been specific reasons for this, which I discuss later in the book. Maybe the underlying source of much of the anger coming out today is not so much the scandals that we have experienced in the last few years but the whole residue of hurt that has accumulated over generations in which the Church exercised power over the people. We priests were on pedestals, put there by the people, and remaining there by our own choice. We were considered by the people to be especially holy and good-living, and we allowed that illusion to continue. We, in a sense, revelled in the power and prestige of our position. We had become the clerical caste. Maybe we not only deserve, but also need, the buffeting we are getting today.

But first I must look at how it came to be that I chose this profession in life.

2

LEARNING AND UNLEARNING ABOUT GOD

Looking back on my life till now, I can see that I spent the bulk of the second part of it trying to unlearn aspects of the religious training of the first part. For people not acquainted with priests and the real nature of their lives that might sound like an extraordinary thing to say and that it is a most unsuitable state for a priest to be in. But in fact being a priest or, more probably, having a theological training helped. It meant that I had a basis on which to rethink my religious attitudes and gradually begin to relearn them. First of all I had to learn quickly not to impose the view of God and His relationship with us that I had developed through my own upbringing on other people in my preaching and ministry generally. This turned out to be relatively easy, since, after my years in theology, I had the intellectual knowledge necessary to readjust my attitudes.

It is a commonly held assumption that you cannot preach with conviction what you have not come to know and experience in your own life. I have learned, both from my own experience and from observing other priests, that this is not the case. In fact to some degree it is the opposite that is more likely to be true. Priests can often preach with most conviction about the things they most lack in their own lives, in the area of either faith or morals. It is, I believe, out of a position of personal weakness and inadequacy that a priest can preach best, because then he is in less danger of becoming dogmatic and talking down to people. While I succeeded in unlearning my religious beliefs for preaching purposes, the process of integrating such unlearning and relearning into my own life was much slower and more difficult, because it involved facing deeply ingrained emotional attitudes and responses. There is no end to the relearning of the things of childhood. You think you have sorted it all out and then along comes some crisis or problem and you are amazed to find yourself responding in the old way again.

Religion played a big part in my life from my earliest memories. Both my mother and father were traditional Catholics who combined a degree of piety with strong ambition for their children. At a later stage the religious fervour and the ambition came together to ensure that all their children got a good education, and they did not put any obstacle in the way when each of us in turn chose to enter religious life. At a still later stage both of them in their separate ways began to look differently at life and religion and, before they died, struggled with a much more complex and questioning view of reality than they had in our youth.

The setting of our local church, a little building by a river, is an idyllic spot to me today. With its small and picturesque bridge, its rural graveyard with the ruin of the old church at the rear and holding the graves of both my parents, it is a haven of peace and tranquillity. While it was a beautiful place in my youth it had another connotation for me then. It was the place where a fairly grim message about life was conveyed. I was a Mass server in those days, and serving Mass was a job of some importance. The old Latin Mass began with the call to come to the altar of God:

Introibo at altare Dei,
Ad Deum qui laetificat juventutem meum.
(I will go unto the altar of God,
To God who is the joy of my youth.)

He wasn't. It wasn't joy that the God I was introduced to back then brought to my youth. There was a strong element of fear associated with that God and also a heavy sense of duty. Religion laid out a life before me in which the stakes were high and the obligations many and varied; there was very little prospect of fun or enjoyment. This life was a very serious business, in which we battled with the Devil to achieve our salvation. The Devil with his wickedness and snares was very powerful and he, as the prayer at the end of Mass said, 'wandered through the world for the ruin of souls.'

And the ruin of one's soul was a frightening prospect, because it involved eternal damnation. I don't know how often I heard sermons on the sufferings of Hell but they were certainly the ones that made most impression on me. One second in the flames of Hell contained more suffering than all the sufferings of this life, but that would go on forever. I can remember many a preacher trying to explain to us what that 'forever' meant. It was horrible. Writing about it now I can still feel the sense of entrapment, of unbearable claustrophobia, that would rise up in me listening to those sermons. And Hell seemed to be the most likely eventuality for us, because the struggle with the Devil was an unequal one. He was devious and smart and constantly on the lookout to trap us. There were so many ways in which he could get us, so many ways in which the dreaded mortal sin could be committed.

A friend of mine recalls from her catechism of those days a sketch of the three states of the human soul. In the first part the soul free from sin is depicted as a child dressed in pristine white with her guardian angel having his arms around her, smiling brightly. The second part depicts the soul in venial sin. The dress is now stained, and the angel has retreated some distance, holding his hands back from the child as a symbol of some withdrawal, while in the corner the Devil can be seen peeping in and leering. The final part of the sketch depicts the soul in mortal sin. The dress is now filthy; the guardian angel is in the distance, head buried in his hands, while the triumphant Devil embraces the sinner as he leads her off to Hell. The reason the struggle with the Devil appeared an unequal one was that he was presented as close by and active, while God was distant and remote. God stood apart, in judgement rather than in love, observing our struggle and adding up the score. I never got the sense as a child that He was on our side in the battle. Our Lady was and the saints were but not God. His job was to judge and his judgement would be done coldly and dispassionately or maybe even in anger. Each night in bed I prayed: 'I must die; I do not know when nor how nor where. But if I die in mortal sin I know I am lost forever. Have mercy on me.'

The priests I had most experience of in my childhood, the men who served in turn as curates at my end of the little country parish, were both quiet men who did not mix very much with us. They did their duties faithfully but otherwise kept a lot to themselves. Neither of them was much of a preacher, and often to our great relief they would skip the sermon on a Sunday. The parish priest was a different character, made of much sterner stuff, who gave short pithy sermons, mainly of a moralistic nature, but he seldom came to our end of the parish. My real experience of sermons was whenever we attended the church attached to the local Redemptorist monastery and the fathers preached or when these same men arrived to give us a parish mission. In contrast to our local curate, the missioners could preach with great colour and power. They had strong voices, developed over years of proclamation in the large churches and cathedrals of the cities. In our little church, and in our imaginations, their voices resounded and dominated everything. One man, with a particularly powerful voice, used to look at the window as he spoke, as if he needed much greater space than our church provided in order to proclaim all that was within him.

It was undoubtedly these preachers who left the deepest impression on me. They tended to be, by our standards, fairly colourful characters. They had travelled a great deal and they could tell stories about faraway countries. This lent an element of mystique and attractiveness to them. I'm sure this is part of what enticed me to this way of life. They were also at the time men of great power. They could dictate to people about the most intimate areas of their lives and they could hold over them the ultimate sanction of damnation. Many of these men were good, gentle people, who treated us with respect and affection but inevitably there was the occasional one who abused the power invested in him.

An old woman from Waterford recently told me of her memory of a mission when she was ten years of age, in a small country church in a very poor part of the county. It was between the two great wars, and the people in this area were simple, largely uneducated, and had to work very hard on the land to make even a subsistence living. There was one woman in the community who, as the saying goes, was not the full shilling. One night at the mission, when the preacher was in full flight at a very serious part of his talk, she, either oblivious to what was going on around her, or affected by the tension in the church, began to laugh. The preacher lost his temper and in a fit of fury, as the woman who was telling me the story remembers it, he put a curse on the people and told them they would all be damned. In today's world that type of behaviour from a preacher would draw down the laughter and derision it deserves but in those times it was deadly serious. The woman told me how she remembered the neighbours gathering into her parent's house that evening in a state of shock, and saying to each other: 'What more can we do?'

Parish missions were held every four or five years and they were community events. Everybody was expected to be there and if my memory serves me right they did attend. It would have been difficult not to. Both the social and religious pressures to be present were very strong. There was one old man who lived alone at the edge of the large stretch of bog in our locality, which was being worked by Bord na Móna. For whatever reason, and I was too young to understand, he did not attend church. Stories abounded of the efforts various missioners had made to confront him and 'save his soul'. But he was a wily character, and was consistently on the lookout during mission time. When he saw the missioner coming he slipped out the back and hid in the enormous spaces of the bog. One especially zealous missioner arrived at the house equipped with wellingtons, and set off chasing the old man over the reeks and the bogholes. Since the missioner was much younger he eventually caught up with the recalcitrant and grounded him with a rugby tackle in the heather. And in that position the old man 'made his peace with God.' Whether that story and similar ones are true or apocryphal, they added greatly to the mystique of the missioners.

The task of people during the mission, apart from being present at the various services, was to 'attend to their duties'. That meant going to confession and receiving Holy Communion. Confession was the big event. The missioners spent many hours in the box and the people queued up outside. I have since learned much about the experience from the priest's point of view and I will write more about it in another part of this book. We have lived to see the style of confession practised then decline almost out of existence. I'm sure it had some therapeutic value but it was a difficult experience for most people. What stands out for me now is the amount of control that was invested in the confessor, especially in the context of a mission, and how the priest had the power to inquire into private areas of a person's life.

Still there was a basic common sense in people which tended to reassert itself gradually and put some balance on the excesses of the time. I remember one of the missions of my youth. There was, as was usual, an older and a younger missioner. It must have been the summer time of the year because it was a bright evening after the mission service.

My father was in intense conversation with some of the younger men outside the church. I moved closer to listen. I did not fully understand what they were saying then but now in memory I can understand it. The young men were going to confession and since they had to confess 'company keeping', as it was known at the time, they decided to go to the young missioner in the hope that he would be more open-minded and understanding. The contrary was the case. They were roundly abused and told that they would have to stop this evil activity. My father suggested to them that they may have chosen the wrong missioner. So one was appointed to try out the older man, while the others waited outside. After a short interval he emerged, all smiles, to tell his story. After he had confessed to the priest that he was going with a girl, he got a gentle talk on the need to love her, and of the intrinsic value of human love. There was an instant queue outside the old man's box and he had a busy week.

My earliest memory of missions was, as a very small boy, being brought to meet the missioner. Outside the door of the sacristy my mother wiped my face with her handkerchief and the missioner came out and patted me on the head. I must have been about six years of age, and it was only a brief moment, but still it stands out in my mind, as if it was an event of great significance. And maybe it was.

Religion in my youth was a very mixed experience. There was a lot that was good about it. Along with sport and the local bog where most of the men worked and where we all saved the turf in the summer and got a chance to earn some much needed money, the church was the other great focus of community activity. It brought us together and was a big part of our shared experience. It also opened our minds to the world of mystery. And it ensured that we were reared with strong moral principles, some of which I have come to appreciate very much in the course of my life. We were taught the importance of discipline and self-control. We learned to value and appreciate simple things. But I would consider the most valuable thing of all that we imbibed from our religious training was a sense of idealism, the importance of service and of caring for people more needy than ourselves. The hard drive of personal ambition that is such a feature of modern society was not as commonly accepted in our youth. The Christian philosophy of loving others was still strong enough to take the hard edge off our ambitions and balance them with a more caring mentality.

I was also, as far as I can remember, a fervent young boy. Each Saturday morning I cycled the four miles to the monastery church to attend the novena to the Mother of Perpetual Succour. I joined with considerable enthusiasm and vehemence in the novena prayer: 'O Mother of Perpetual Succour, behold me a miserable sinner at thy feet. I have recourse to thee and put my trust in thee. O Mother of mercy, have pity on me.' Later in life I met a woman who suffered from a poor self-image, and who blamed her problems on the constant recitation of that prayer when she was a child. 'A few occasions every week I knelt at the shrine,' she said, 'and I looked up at the picture and proclaimed myself a "miserable sinner". I think I came to believe it too deeply.' Her comments resonated with me. It is this aspect of my religious upbringing that I most regret and that I have struggled to unlearn. We were taught to think badly of ourselves. Instead of focusing on the goodness of God, which is where all Christian teaching should begin, we were first told of our own sinfulness. And the emphasis on sexual sin, which I deal with elsewhere, led us to be ill at ease in our own bodies.

Two spiritual writers dominated my religious training in secondary boarding school. They were an unlikely pair. A classic fifteenth-century treatise called *The Imitation of Christ* by Thomas à Kempis, and a sentimental eighteenth-century Italian book on Our Lady, *The Glories of Mary* by Alphonsus Liguori. They were not the only religious input but the reason they dominated was due to sheer repetition. Thomas à Kempis was read every morning during breakfast:

> Your time here is very short: take another look at the way in which you spend it . . .
>
> At every turn of your life, keep the end in view; remember that you will have to stand before a strict judge, who knows everything, who cannot be won over by gifts or talked around by excuses, who will give you your deserts . . .
>
> It is a happy man that understands what is meant by loving Jesus and by despising oneself for his sake.

It was an extraordinary choice for breakfast reading for a group of teenagers in the early sixties. True, it is a classic spiritual book but it was written many centuries ago and aimed specifically at religious. In other words, it was intended for people who were advanced both in age and in spiritual understanding. For it to make any sense to boys of the second half of the twentieth century it would have needed a great deal of interpreting. Instead, we got it undiluted each morning with our porridge!

The evening meal each day began with a reading from *The Glories of Mary*. Something similar to the following:

> Let us, then, have recourse, and always have recourse, to this most sweet queen, if we would be certain of our salvation: as she herself said to St Bridget: 'Therefore miserable will he be, and miserable will he be to all eternity, who, in this life, having it in his power to invoke me, who am so compassionate to all, and so desirous to assist sinners, is miserable enough not to invoke me and so is damned.'

Again, this is one of the classic books on Our Lady. But it is a book of its time and place: southern Italy in the middle of the eighteenth century. The style is florid and in the modern phrase somewhat over the top. It could have contributed to our education and our devotion to Our Lady, but only with careful interpretation and explanation. I often wonder what type of mentality was behind the choosing of these two books as our daily reading. I know they had been read for generations in that school and there was a certain element of the unthinking about it. Weren't they classics and hadn't they proved the test of time! I believe they were utterly unsuitable. It is impossible to measure what effect, if any, they had on us. They became part of the air we breathed and as such had substantial effect. Both of them are heavy, serious books with a lot of theological content and focus mainly on eternity. Religious belief should be presented to young people in a much lighter and more lively fashion, with an emphasis on the richness and depth that it can give to living this life and the happiness that can be attained through having a faith. Reflecting on death, eternity and salvation are more appropriate to a later stage in life, when people have come to know for themselves the emptiness of so much of human ambition. In today's world the competitive nature of the education system and the intense pressure of exams is to some extent robbing young people of their youth and forcing an adult seriousness on them at too early an age. Something of the same thing was done to our generation by feeding us a too adult and serious, and sometimes even doom-laden, version of spirituality.

Yet, at the end of my five years at that school I decided to join the Redemptorists. Since my two brothers had already gone ahead of me there was something of the conveyer belt about it, I suppose. But there was more than that. One moment stands out for me. It was my last year in school during the final retreat in Holy Week. A classmate and good friend, Paddy Fitzgerald from south Kerry, and myself were chatting about our future. He was an only boy in a family with three sisters. His father was dead and he was very close to the other members of the family. He had great energy for life and loved sport, especially football. I remember what he said to me that day: 'A big part of me does not want to be a priest. I hate having to give up so much. But somehow I feel that I must. I feel I am being called.' That was a common enough attitude in those days. We were constantly told that God chose certain people, that he called them specifically to the priesthood and that it was of crucial importance to answer that call. Not to do so would be a rejection of God. I felt that I too was being called.

The noviciate was the first introduction to a religious community. It lasted for thirteen months and was intended as a period of intense spiritual preparation and training. The form of noviciate that I participated in was based on centuries of tradition in Christianity. It has since been largely discontinued and the new form of training bears little enough resemblance to what we had and comes at a later stage in the years of training. The form of religious formation today that has most in common with our style of noviciate is that used by the fundamentalist sects and cults. Our training did not create the same type of uneasiness among family or society in general, because religious life had social status. It was accepted as a good way of living, while the cults are regarded as dangerous because of the brainwashing they practise.

I find it very difficult to recall much of my noviciate now. It has become something of a blur in my mind. I must have gone through it in a state of shock or in some form of semi-comatose boredom. Putting a seventeen-year-old into a black suit and a flannelette shirt to which a white collar was attached and requiring him to wear a black tie and a black hat on his head, seem today quite ridiculous things to do. But it did not seem so strange in those days. I remember saying goodbye to my sporting companions at the crossroads as I was being driven over to the monastery to enter and feeling the strangeness of the way that I was dressed compared to them. For good and all I was being set apart and I felt then for the first time the loneliness of the choice I was making for myself in life.

The noviciate was a completely enclosed year, during which we had two visits from our families and a minimum of contact with the outside world. Our novice master was a fanatical walker, so he took us for walks around the roads a few days a week. We walked in threes, to prevent any kind of exclusive friendship developing. We must have seemed a strange sight, twelve young men, scarcely more than boys, walking the roads in black suits, with black hats on our heads. I hated walking in those days because I regarded it as a waste of good playing time. We were allowed the occasional game of football, which was the highlight for me, though it must have been a punishment for some of my companions who were in no way sporting. One of the central ideas of the noviciate was that the group did everything together. There were twelve of us to begin with, and we ended the year with nine. So our games were five or six a side. In all my years of sport I have never played any game with the intensity with which I played those football matches with my fellow novices. There were only four of us who had any proficiency at the game and we normally marked each other, while the rest were largely spectators. I remember being spoken to by the novice master over the seriousness and the aggression of my play. It was a measure both of the smallness of our world and of the desperate need for some sort of outlet for pent-up energy.

A story was passed down from previous years about how three novices had got into a fight on the football field and blows were struck, leading one man to appear at evening prayer with a black eye. He was spotted by the novice master and an investigation began. The first person to be questioned was the zealator. The zealator was appointed by the novice master, normally on the basis of seniority, to serve for a period of six months. His function was to observe the behaviour of his fellow novices and report all deviations from the rule to the novice master. A tribunal of inquiry was set up, and eventually the truth was unearthed. The book of canon law was duly opened and the part read out where it stated that to strike a cleric was a serious crime, punishable by excommunication. The three young men were sent to bed thinking that not only their short-term but also their long-term – and indeed their eternal – future was in jeopardy. Until it dawned on one of them in the middle of the night that a novice, being a trainee, was not yet a cleric and therefore could be struck without such dire consequences.

Apart from the walks and football, prayer and work were the two big features of life there and most of each day was spent in silence. We were introduced to the notion of meditation and did three half-hour sessions every day, in the morning and in the evening in the chapel and, most difficult of all, a half an hour in the afternoon alone in your room. I remember kneeling in my room on fine summer afternoons vainly attempting to pray. We were admonished that we shouldn't look out the window but observe what was called modesty of the eyes. Yet many a day I stood looking longingly out at the green fields and wishing to race over them with a football or hurley in my hands. I must have wondered what I was doing there. I do not know if I seriously thought of leaving during that year. I can distinctly picture a scene from some time during the year: myself and a friend sitting on a concrete step leading up one of the hills in the grounds of the monastery and saying to each other: 'What in the name of God are we doing here?'

Whether that was just a passing mood or something deeper I am not sure. What was the motivation that kept me there? I know that we were strongly encouraged not to turn our backs on our vocation and were warned that if we did St Alphonsus would personally accuse us on the day of judgement. In his book, *The True Spouse*, which we were reading at the time, he railed against those early companions who left or, as he said, deserted their vocation. Invariably they came to a bad end, being stabbed to death by the husbands of the women who had led them astray, or other similar types of misfortune. Was it that threat that kept me in or had I a stronger, more positive motivation? I don't know. There was, inevitably, some element of drifting along. It was an enclosed world, with its own calendar of events, of feast days and celebrations, of days of penance and fasting, of highs and lows, even the occasional outing to the beach in summer, which absorbed you and kept you going.

Penance was a big feature of life there; indeed I presume the whole year was intended as a form of penance, in order to prepare a person for the rigour and discipline of the priestly life. Still, being introduced to some of the particular forms of penance that were practised was something of a shock. The most shocking of all was the one that was known as the discipline. The first time I stood in line in the corridor, took down my pants, and began to beat myself on the backside with a whip was one of the strangest sensations I have ever had in my life. In fact some of the other penances were more painful, because the degree of pain inflicted by the discipline depended totally on the amount of vigour with which you used it and, since it was done in semi-darkness, nobody monitored the power of the lash you administered to yourself. The wearing of what was called a 'cilice' was more difficult. A cilice was a steel chain wrapped tightly around either your arm or your thigh, with sharp points sticking into the flesh. Wearing the leg cilice all morning, through meditation, Mass, thanksgiving and breakfast could be quite a difficult experience. It was very hard to walk while wearing it. Nowadays, if we heard of a cult doing the type of things I am describing (common to most religious orders of that era) the media would discuss them for days on end. Experts in psychology would be brought in to explain the hidden motivation behind them and consider the damage they would do to the individuals. They would have great fun drawing all sorts of conclusions about sexually perverted attitudes from the practice of the discipline!

At the end of the year we introduced the new novices to the regime, and I can still see the shocked look on the face of one of them when I explained to him about the discipline. While the cilice could be more painful, I think the discipline did more psychological damage to us. The fact that it involved stripping and involved *that* part of the body were giving a very negative message. There are areas of privacy and intimacy in life that most of us find some difficulty in integrating into the rest of our personality at the best of times. I can see now that there was generally a very strong message being given in all of this about our bodies. It came out of a theology that saw the human person consisting of two distinct entities, body and soul. The soul was all that was important and that is why there was so much emphasis put on preparing for eternity. The body was seen as bad, in that it was the source of all the troublesome passions, and as such it needed to be controlled. The way to do that was through discipline and penance. Rather ironically because the food was very good and there was a great shortage of the sort of vigorous exercise that I had always engaged in, I put on two stone during that year!

All of what I have described was done under the name of formation. Today I would say that there was far too much mind-control going on. That is why I said that this system is most replicated now in the modern cults and the way in which they 'love-bomb' their recruits. We were cut off from our families; all letters, going in and out, were monitored. We were not allowed to use the telephone; access to newspapers, radio or television was very seldom permitted and even then only for special, usually religious, events. The result was that we had no real contact with the outside world. With prayer and spiritual reading we spent six to seven hours each day in specifically religious activity. We were warned that to leave the congregation would be to risk losing our souls and it was in this context we had to decide about making our first profession. It could not be said to have been a freely chosen commitment.

Of what use was that year as a preparation for life? I find it very difficult to say since my memory of it is so unclear. I have always tended to think of it as a negative rather than a positive influence on me and regard it as part of the baggage that I later had to discard. Perhaps that is not fully fair to the purpose of the year and to the people who were in charge of us then. It did serve as something of a cut-off point, where the old way of life that we had lived at home was sharply, almost cruelly, terminated and a new way of life, very different, and, we were told, superior in the eyes of God, was embarked upon. In that sense it was almost like starting life afresh. The notion of conversion that is prevalent in the Catholic faith, of leaving the past behind and starting out on a new way, was being implemented here. The new life would be a life of self-denial, of sacrifice, lived in the service of others. It was very idealistic and as such had a great appeal to the young mind but there was an unreality about it from many points of view.

I have since learned a great deal about the notion of conversion. It is a very powerful concept and has a strong base in the Scriptures. It happens when a person contemplates life and decides to leave behind some of the beliefs and behaviour patterns that he or she has been living by and instead takes on a new way of living based on different principles and attitudes. Because of the privileged position that priesthood gives, I have been able to observe and sometimes even to facilitate many conversions. I am not at all talking about converting to Catholicism but of conversion in the deeper sense of change of life. I have known people who were addicted to alcohol and whose lives were in a mess, decide one day that they could no longer control their situation and looked for help. From that day on they began to live in a new way. I have seen couples whose marriage was on the rocks decide, sometimes with help, to look at where they were going wrong and gradually develop a new way of relating to each other. I have known this to grow into a fresh and deep relationship between them and constitute a new beginning. I have seen people who lived for the making of money begin gradually to rethink their priorities and to change from being greedy to being generous. This is the type of thing that is meant by conversion. Essential to conversion is first of all to have lived in the world, to have tasted the hardship and difficulty of life and developed the ability to recognise and the humility to admit to mistakes and failure.

Neither does conversion happen without a person's

coming to know and experience pain and suffering. And it does not come easily, or, in most cases, quickly. It involves great struggle and effort. Any change in lifestyle or attitude involves that. The mistake of our system of training was that it was trying to convert us before we had lived. It was trying to impose on young, immature people who had not yet begun to live in any real sense of the word the powerful notion of changing their lives. It was trying to short-circuit years of living and hard-earned experience. It could not possibly succeed. I think that is why I look back now on my noviciate year, and find so much of it is a blank, so hard for me to measure its significance. If it had come at a much later stage in life, and then inevitably in a very different form, it would have been more beneficial. Many people, religious or not, when they reach a certain stage in their lives, would appreciate the value of days spent in silence, the opportunity to read, the time to spend in prayer or in reflection.

It did influence our lives but it was an imposed structure of thought and behaviour. It had not, and could not possibly have, any real inner conviction underpinning it. We left there, in theory and in appearance, as people who had taken on a whole new way of life but we had yet to live the old life; we had yet to find ways of releasing all the bursting energy that was inside us; we had yet to find expression for our personalities and to come to understand the type of people we were becoming at this stage of rapid development in our emotional and psychological lives. About the realities of life as such we were largely ignorant. And yet we were 'converted'. We had begun the journey of the spiritual life at the end rather than the beginning.

And yet I continued. The seminary years were more open and in many ways enjoyable and exciting. Most of my companions left at different points along the way. I saw the numbers in the seminary go from almost one hundred to less than forty in the space of a few years. Was it the courageous ones who stayed despite all the upheaval or was the decision to leave the one that involved most courage? Were we, the ones who stayed, the real cowards? How can we answer those questions now! Is the answer of any importance any more? Some went and some stayed. That is the reality. During the period of my training, which lasted in all for ten years, my motivation for staying changed many times. It wasn't in any sense easy or smooth. There were many times when I wondered if I was in the right place. None of that uncertainty should be surprising when you consider all that was happening both inside the seminary and in society at large during those years. I remember clearly the time that one of my older brothers, who was also in the seminary, decided to leave. I must have been in my second year at the time. I know that part of me greatly envied him as he walked out that door.

After about six years I reached a major crisis. I had come into serious conflict with my superior. We just did not see eye to eye on anything and communication had largely broken down between us. He had introduced a system by which each student should spend two years away from the seminary and be involved in some form of apostolic work in order to help him to mature and make a final decision. It was a good innovation though we did not think so at the time. We were tired of being students and the thought of two more years, even if spent outside the seminary, was not attractive. We wanted to get the whole thing over, be ordained and settle into our life's work. My superior felt that what I needed was two years out working on our foreign mission in Brazil. He clearly believed that a while in the bush would put manners on me. Relations were so bad between us at the time that the very fact that he wanted this made me a vehement opponent of it. He said that I could either agree to go to Brazil or leave the seminary. I chose to leave and the decision was made. I remember the first person I informed of my decision was my friend Paddy, who had moved on ahead of me in the seminary, was due to be ordained shortly and had been appointed to go to Brazil after ordination.

He was, of course, disappointed to hear my story and we sat for a long time discussing the situation and, as we tended to do in those days, smoking endless cigarettes. Then there was a knock on the door and I was summoned again to the superior. He was a very fair man and he had been considering the situation. He explained that since communication had broken down between us he felt that it would be good to get the opinion of a third person before a final decision would be reached. So he asked me to see a visiting theologian. After discussion with him a compromise was reached: it was decided that I should spend the next two years teaching in our school in Limerick, the one I myself had attended. It was going through a major change into an ordinary secondary school and there would be time for me to think over my future. My friend Paddy was ordained, went to Brazil and he, who was reared beside the sea and was an excellent swimmer, was drowned within a short time as he swam one day in a swollen river.

It was during those few years spent in Limerick that I made my final decision to continue in religious life and be ordained. It was during the early seventies and the monastery where I was living was a hive of activity and vitality. Renewal was in the air and there was a sense that a new Church and a new congregation were coming into being. I was caught up in the excitement of it all. It seemed the challenge was great and the opportunities endless.

3

Sex and Celibacy

Celibacy is compulsory for priests in the Catholic Church. Historically this was not always so and many people believe that it will not be too long before it becomes optional again. I don't know how many priests choose celibacy with enthusiasm or how many just accept it as part of the package. They want to be priests and this is part of the price they have to pay. For me as a religious the situation is somewhat different. It is one of the vows that religious take and as such it could generally be said that religious make a more free choice in this area. At least that is the theory of the situation. In practice I am not sure. It is interesting to look back now, and see how well my family and social background, and my religious training, moulded me in such a manner as to make the 'free' choice almost automatic.

I presume I was not unusual for my time, when I say that I grew up in a home where sex was never mentioned or discussed. In the days before television and when people had only a limited access to radio and newspapers, both of which were carefully censored both in the public domain and in the home, there were none of the type of sexual elements that are so commonplace today. In the area of sex

I was, throughout my youth, incredibly innocent, and I retained my innocence to an age that would be inconceivable today. Yet a great many of my attitudes to sex were associated with guilt. That is probably not surprising when you consider that Catholic moral theology, or at least the version we were taught at the time, asserted that even the slightest sexual thought, as long as it was 'entertained' or 'indulged in' deliberately, was enough to condemn a person to Hell for all eternity. Catholic morality was not the sole reason for my guilt. I have come to understand this in recent years as I have reflected on a childhood experience.

We are hearing so much about child sexual abuse today, as all its secret evil is coming out into the open. We've become used to the tabloids describing the latest abuser to be unmasked as a 'beast' or a 'demon'. But the man who sexually abused me when I was a child of seven or eight did not appear to me to be either of those things. I would not have described him then as an 'abuser', though I would certainly use that word about him now. Instead I remember him as being very gentle. He did not use any physical force in getting me to come to him. Rather did he lure and entice me by his gentleness, and by the reward of half a crown (a lot of money for a young country child in the fifties) for each occasion. It is an interesting fact that even though I used to hand over the half-crown to my mother, telling her it was a gift from this man, she never seemed to wonder why he was being so generous. Yet she was very protective of my sister. On one occasion a man gave my sister a gift of a shilling, and when she told my mother she was strongly warned never to take money from a strange man again. So, clearly she was aware of the danger of a young girl being abused but it did not enter her head that it might happen to a little boy. The abuser was employed in the local Bord na Móna works and lived in one of the Nissen huts that had been erected during the war to house the workers when there was no means of transport to and from the job.

Education and experience have helped me to understand more about the means by which the human mind can blot out uncomfortable realities. I know that happened to me. Even to this day, there is a lot that I cannot remember. For instance, how did this man get me into the hut? How did he manage to separate me from the other children? How often did it happen? It may have been as few as half a dozen times or it may have been many more. I have no way now of being sure. I know there was no penetrative sex, because he never caused me any physical hurt. He was so gentle and reassuring in his manner. When I try to remember how I felt at the time about it, I have even more difficulty recalling my feelings. I know it exercised my mind and I worried a great deal about it but, needless to say, in the climate of those times I did not talk to anyone. When adults never mentioned the subject, there somehow was no permission or no opportunity for children to bring it up.

Maybe I shouldn't blame the times completely, because I understand that many children even today do not tell when they are being abused. It is hard for a child to find the words to describe what is happening. I can remember struggling with the sense of being used, though I wouldn't have been naming it like this, even in my own mind. I tried to comfort myself with the knowledge that while he exposed my nakedness, he was also exposing his own, and this equalised the embarrassment. I know differently now. Considering the age he was then, I presume the man is now long dead. The huts were closed down shortly afterwards, because with the advent of the motor car and better public transport they were no longer needed, and he moved away. I had no further contact with him. He was clearly a paedophile and he had found the ideal location in which to exercise his paedophilia. The huts were situated in the centre of our little village. One of them was turned into a hall, where there were various games which we, the local children, played whenever we could get in. They were adjoining the hurling field and the Bord na Móna works, so we were constantly around the place. In a sense, we were freely at his disposal. And all the silence about sex in the culture of the place made the possibility of his being found out remote. It was a paedophile's paradise.

Boarding school was almost the only option available to us for secondary education at the time. There was a boys' secondary school in a town about ten miles away which a small number of my contemporaries attended. The public transport system which served it was less than adequate, which meant that the travelling students missed part of the first and last class each day. Instead of this option and under the influence of the Redemptorists in the monastery nearby, my brothers and I chose to go as boarders to their small junior seminary in Limerick city, which I referred to in the previous chapter. It was in many ways more benign than most of the boarding-schools of its time. Corporal punish–ment was rarely used and the quality and quantity of the food compared very favourably with the diocesan secondary boarding-schools. While I have a lot of good memories of those years in that school, I look on it as having been far too strong on brainwashing and mind control. Every student who was accepted into the school was presumed to be a candidate for the priesthood in the Redemptorists and the whole system was geared towards preparing him for this from the very beginning at the age of twelve. I am aware that not everybody experienced the place as I did. I have spoken to many former students over the years, and in general those who did not go on to become priests or Redemptorists have a more benign and nostalgic memory of the place than I or many of my fellow Redemptorists. I am not sure why this should be the case but maybe they had the ability to regard the place more lightly and not take the attempts at mind-control so seriously.

In the course of the five years we had a great many conferences, or spiritual lectures or sermons. The president addressed us for half an hour every Sunday morning and we also had many retreats. One of the important things to develop, we were told, was the virtue of purity. 'I give you my body that it may be chaste and pure,' as the prayer said. I learned to hate that word 'purity' and at the same time to feel guilty for hating it. Of course, I was so confused and ignorant about sex in general that I did not understand its meaning but I knew it was something severe and difficult, and that I had a long way to go before I would be pure, if ever. The message I seemed to be getting was that my salvation could well depend on my achieving this elusive virtue. There were two problems at work here. There was my own buried guilt resulting from the abuse a few years earlier. I am now aware that those of us who have been sexually abused have to deal with the problem of a negative self-image, a feeling of being tainted. I think professionals refer to this as the 'damaged-goods' syndrome. There was also a narrow, puritanical and otherworldly version of purity being offered to us, based on the traditional notion of the soul's being the only important thing, and the body the home of all evil passions and desires.

The president of the college was a refined, intellectual man with great strength of personality and though not a tall man he had an imposing presence. He took us for what was called 'colloquium' twice a year. A colloquium was a private conversation with him in his office. This happened during the retreats. These were of three days' duration, held in September and again during Holy Week. They involved total silence, many hours of prayer and the reading of lives of the saints that for the most part were unreal accounts of the lives of the individuals concerned, in that they were over-sentimental, pious and often poorly written. Those retreats were difficult days for all of us but for me, by far the most difficult aspect of the retreat was the colloquium. The reason for this had its origins in my very first colloquium. Since every student had to go in, it invariably involved a fairly lengthy period of queuing outside the room, which served to build up the tension and create a knot in the stomach.

The president was seated behind a large desk and he brought me in behind the desk to sit beside him and he put his arm around my shoulder in what he presumably intended to be a fatherly gesture but which made me decidedly uncomfortable. Then he proceeded to quiz me about whether I had any 'bad' thoughts, about something he called 'urges' and whether I ever 'did anything with myself'. I have still got a clear memory of the embarrassment of it all, of the awful sense of entrapment, of confusion and of shame! I can understand now why I had all this jumble of emotions. Deep down I was feeling: 'He knows about me; he knows what I have been up to.' And to confirm my worst suspicions he asked: 'Did anything ever happen to you?' I know that he was trying to be helpful but it did not work with me. I felt like a criminal who had been caught out and I lied through my teeth. 'No, certainly not. Nothing at all.' There was a long, long silence and then he repeated the question, and I gave an even more vehement denial. He let me go but now I had a real problem. Not only had I done these terrible things but he knew about them! I knew that my denial had not convinced him. How did he know? Was the mark of the sinner on my face or something? I dreaded every colloquium from then on in case he would return to the same topic.

Apart from this guilt and the fear of being found out, I cannot remember having any great sexual struggles during my years in the secondary school. I was a fanatic for sport, and in the best boarding-school tradition the authorities believed in the value of plenty of exercise and cold showers to dampen down the passions and use up the excess energy. In many ways they were good years, with great companion-ship and camaraderie among us. It was a small, tightly-run school, so there weren't any of the nasty elements of the larger boarding-schools, like bullying. But the guiding attitudes were narrow and limited about life in general and sexuality in particular.

About half-way through my time in the school, probably during my third year, I got into further trouble in this respect. We used to spend long hours in a large room we called the study hall. At the top of it were some toilets and each of them had an entrance which consisted of a little lobby area with a radiator. A young classmate from Cork and myself got into the habit of occasionally slipping up to the toilet, putting our bottoms up against the radiator in the lobby and having a chat. Somebody, obviously with a much more knowledgeable and devious mind than we had, reported our activity to the president. I was summoned to the seat behind the desk. On this occasion there was no arm round my shoulder. He was clearly very angry but was, I can see now, much too controlled and repressed in himself to allow his anger to be expressed in any ordinary way. Instead, in the best Catholic tradition, his technique was guilt-provoking: 'I am very disappointed in you, I who trusted you so much.' (I have ever since detested criticism that couched itself in guilt-provoking language. I remember reacting very angrily in later years, when I was a young priest, to an older Redemptorist who disapproved of a stand I was taking on a particular issue and who began his talk with me by saying: 'I knew your father, and he was a gentleman . . . ')

I was utterly baffled. I knew that having a chat during study was forbidden but I didn't expect it to generate so much disapproval. While he was hinting at some awful misdemeanour, he was making no effort to explain to me exactly what I had done wrong. I was at best very vague about sex in its normal manifestation and, in spite of my own earlier experience, I had little clue that deviations from the norm were possible. I presume that he eventually realised my state of innocence and he sent me from the room with a caution, but without explaining the reason for his displeasure. It was only when, a few days later, one of my fellow students explained some things to me, that I had any indication of what I was being accused of. I was amazed at the thought that the little lobby of the toilet, with its precious radiator, could be used for activities other than discussing the prospects of Cork and Galway hurling. These were things about which I had never dreamed and which seemed to me both disturbing and somewhat revolting.

My experience of colloquia with the president ended as it began. On the occasion of my last one, which was at Easter in my final year just before I did my Leaving Cert when I was seventeen years of age and held the exalted position of head boy in the school, he decided to go through with me the 'facts of life', drawing little diagrams on a page in front of him. Did he do this with every student at this stage or was I a particularly innocent or confused one? Had he his arm around my shoulder as he did it or had that ceased as I got bigger? How much of what he was telling me had I known already? I do not know the answers to these question but I do know that when he finished his explanations and when he asked me had I any questions, if my life depended on it I would not have been able to ask one. It was not a pleasant moment. He finished with the same question he had asked me in first year: had anything happened to me? This time I said yes, it had. I cannot remember how much I told him about it, but I do remember his response: 'Now don't you feel relieved, having got all that off your chest?' I didn't. Just relieved to get out of there, and never to have to sit and discuss anything with him again.

In some sense he was, in my eyes, the embodiment of purity, something that I had been told was so important and that I would never attain. And yet I had another, very different, feeling about him, which I have only been able to put into words in recent years. He was an upright man and

I am not suggesting that there was anything untoward in his attitude towards me but he became linked in my mind with the abuser. He too had trapped me, sitting in that chair behind his big desk. He had, in my eyes, also uncovered my privacy and my shame. He had left me exposed and naked, and feeling guilty about myself. I don't mean to be harsh or judgemental of him. He undoubtedly meant well, and was trying to do his best. He did not have the advantage of modern knowledge or the sort of skills that counsellors acquire in their training today. He hadn't read Carl Rogers with his notion of non-judgemental listening, or any of the other writers whose thinking has become part and parcel of the modern approach to counselling. One good result of the whole experience was to teach me to be very careful, whenever in my work as a priest I have come in contact with a victim of child sexual abuse, about intruding into their private trauma. And I wonder if, even with all modern sensitivity shown, some children still feel the same sense of being abused once more as they are being questioned about what happened to them.

What effect did the sexual abuse have on my life? It is so difficult to measure. I do tend to get impatient with so much of what is written today which suggests that it can destroy a person's life. I do not feel that my life was destroyed. I was certainly fairly deeply affected and it is only in later years that I have come to understand by how much and how the course of my future life was probably influenced. Guilt was the big legacy – a feeling that I was bad and shameful. Still, growing up in the Ireland of the fifties, especially in a rural part of the west, and greatly influenced by the famed 'hellfire' preachers, the Redemptorists, could I have avoided developing some guilt about sexuality and about my body anyway? And was the degree of guilt that I was burdened with greater then the average? Did I become a priest because of what happened in that Nissen hut? Was this my subconscious way of escaping from sex, trying to assuage my guilt and shame, and placating an angry God? Who knows? And does it matter now? In making our decisions about life we are influenced by a myriad things and since we get just one chance at living we can only do a tiny fraction of the many things that are worth doing. I could have made worse choices and ended up with a lot less satisfying life than I have had. I know I had difficulty coming to terms with sexuality and feeling at home in my body but as far as I can see so have many other people. I have always felt that it is important to move on with life. If we get stuck in any one incident or time and get locked into the trauma of it, it can dominate our whole life. And I know now that in being sexually abused I am not exceptional. Others have had the same experience and, I presume, something of the same struggle in coming to terms with it.

In writing about this, I am conscious that I am exposing myself for a third time. But the big difference now is that, on this occasion, I am in control. It is my own choice and I can reveal as little or as much as I choose. The real evil of abuse is the loss of control. I have thought a lot about what has happened to me and have been lucky enough to have a friend with whom I could discuss it at various stages, and I believe now that I have come to terms with it. People who have known me and for whatever reason might have disapproved of some aspect of my life or attitudes can now say: 'So that is what was wrong with him all along! He was abused and he never really dealt with it. Now it all makes sense!' I can handle that. For me it is part of what has happened in my life. At the time it was important and it has had its effects, whatever they may be. But I have moved on. I have survived. Many other things have happened which have had their effects, for good and bad. And I think I am an all-right type of person and haven't had a bad life. So be it.

My seminary years, from the mid-sixties to the mid-seventies, were the time when the whole world changed. But first there was that year of noviciate about which I have written in another chapter. In the matter of sexuality, suffice it to say that it reinforced a lot of the traditional attitudes in a very powerful way and served to build further layers of repression inside of me. Any belated stirrings of adolescence and sexual awareness that had begun to happen were firmly put under wraps. I remember having a discussion with a fellow novice, who was somewhat more advanced than I, about his difficulty in leaving his girl friend behind him when he entered the noviciate. What I found difficult was leaving behind the joy of competitive sport and I argued with him that I was making a far greater sacrifice than he was in leaving a girl, which to me seemed frivolous and somewhat unmanly.

I recently chatted with a classmate of mine from our village about his experience of those years. He was one of the people who went to the secondary school in the nearby town. It was the heyday of the marquees and he talked about what a big influence that had on him during those years. From April to September, and especially during the summer months, one or two nights each week anything up to fifteen young people would pile into a local car and head off to places like Kiltormer, Portumna or Monivea. They danced with their sisters until they developed some confidence and then they began to spread their wings. It was clearly a much more normal and healthy introduction to relationships and sexuality that I had. I do remember the piling into cars but for me it was to go to hurling and football matches, which I loved. But that too was terminated the day I entered the noviciate.

It took some time for me to re-emerge out of my shell after the year but at least the seminary was a more normal type of environment, with a bit more freedom of thought. I was lucky to be attending university and even though we had, for the first few years until the changes came in, to dress in black, with the full white 'dog' collar around our necks and a black hat on our heads, at least we were meeting with young people of our own age and breathing in the stirrings of revolution that were in the air in all universities at the time. It was the era of the miniskirt and I did gradually begin to notice how attractive and enticing a young woman could be with long silken legs and a jaunty air. It was my third year before I ventured to get involved in a local youth club. On one of my first nights there an affectionate little fifteen-year-old invited me to walk with herself and her younger sister the short journey to her home and meet her parents. As we walked along she held my hand in the natural easy way that she had.

That was one of the few nights in my life that sleep completely eluded me, as I tossed and turned, battling with very powerful emotions that I didn't really understand and had little or no training or resources to cope with. I was both frightened and excited. Living through the emotional stirrings of a thirteen- or fourteen-year-old when you were twenty and in a seminary was a strange and unsettling experience. Not all my fellow seminarians were as naive and backward as I was, however. One of my companions in the youth club was a lot more daring and I, his friend, acted as gooseberry for him on various occasions. I remember driving my father's Austin A40, which I had on loan for the day, from Connemara to Galway as my companion and one of the girls from the club were getting to know each other in the back seat. It was a lucky thing that the road from Spiddal was not as busy then as it is now, since I spent most of the journey looking in the rear mirror! And on another occasion I was again gooseberry to a companion who was courting a local girl on the hill above the beach in the town where we had our holiday house. As they lay together on the ground passionately kissing, her short skirt left little to the imagination from my vantage point just below them. Even though I was over twenty years of age at the time, I remember being disturbed and sexually aroused by this scene. I now know that the conclusion of all that I am saying is that my sexual development was seriously retarded – and that is putting it mildly!

What a ferment of suppressed emotion that seminary must have been in those years of the sixties. I have often wondered since how much homosexual activity there was, though I for one was totally unaware of any at the time. There must have been at least the normal number of gays among us, and probably more. Even those of us who were heterosexual had such little outlet for our feelings that we must have found ourselves being attracted to each other. I know that I went through periods, especially during my first two or three years there, of having very strong feelings, though not ones that I would have identified at the time as sexual, for other students, and being inordinately jealous because they were more friendly with someone else than with me. It was well known and commented on that some of the senior students would take young students under their wings, 'sugar babies' as they were called, and tend to develop a furtively exclusive relationship with them. How far any of that went I have no way of knowing.

Gradually the freedom of attitude and of life outside began to infiltrate our walls and influence our thinking. The system loosened out: we discarded the black clothes; we were allowed to get involved in the social and cultural life of the university; and we even began to venture into the local pubs. In all aspects of life things were changing. I remember a particular retreat day in the seminary. It was normal that on retreat days there would be reading of some spiritual book during meals. It was decided that on this day there would be music instead and, as part of the new thinking about giving students more responsibility over their lives, we were allowed the option of choosing our own music that would be appropriate for the day. It was assumed by the superior that some classical piece or something on a religious theme would be chosen. He expected to eat his meal to the strains of Gounod's 'Ave Maria', or something similar. He hadn't reckoned on our total absorption in the Beatles and Simon and Garfunkel. The tape was switched on, and I could see the surprise on the faces of the older members of the community, while the students smiled and tapped their feet to the rhythms. 'The Sound of Silence' passed off all right;

at least it could be said to be in some way appropriate to a day of retreat, since it was about the value of silence and all that. Even 'Bridge over Troubled Water' was OK. It could be said to have some application to God's working in our lives. But the third song on the tape was 'Cecilia'.

> Oh, Cecilia, you're breaking my heart, you're
>   shaking my confidence daily.
> Oh, Cecilia, I'm down on my knees; I'm
>   begging you please, to come home.

Looks of disapproval from the priest's side of the refectory, but so far, no action.

> Making love in the afternoon with Cecilia, up
>   in my bedroom.
> I got up to wash my face; when I come back to
>   bed, someone's taken my place.

A loud snort of disgust from one of the older priests, and the superior quickly got up and turned off the tape recorder. The meal continued in total silence, but with many an amused glance on our side of the room.

Celibacy is part of the package that goes with priesthood. In my experience there are few enough, even among religious, and a lot fewer among the diocesan priesthood, who choose celibacy for its own sake. Rather they accept it, with varying degrees of enthusiasm, as part of the price they have to pay for being a priest or religious. It is not a subject we discuss among ourselves with any degree of openness, so it is difficult to know what the real story of celibate living is for the average priest. My experience in talking to priests at a counselling level would suggest that for many of the older generation it involved a constant struggle with sexual thoughts, fantasies and the temptation to masturbate.

In my later years in the seminary there was quite a dramatic change in the thinking on this subject and in the type of approach to be adopted towards living the celibate life. This change came about mostly through the advances in knowledge of human psychology and the development of our understanding of the human person. The traditional way of dealing with the problems that celibacy caused in the life of a priest was to avoid all 'occasions of sin' and to say your prayers. If you kept well away from any type of relationship or even contact with women beyond the minimum necessary, you would be safe. The old theology reinforced all this with dire threats of what would happen in the next life if you failed to live up to your vow. This is where the struggle with the fantasies and the thoughts came in. All of these were regarded as seriously sinful, indeed as mortal sins in many cases.

I have met many priests who are very scrupulous in this area and worry excessively over the smallest of things. All through their lives they have carried on a massive struggle with their own physical desires, which they have regarded as bad and the work of the Devil. This has led them to become almost split personalities, living comfortably in their intellectual lives but so repressed in their emotions and so frightened by them as to be very damaged human beings. The theology and spirituality of the time which emphasised the body-soul split reinforced this feeling. The body and everything to do with it, and most especially the sexual nature, was bad and sinful. How many priests and religious have lived lives of constant struggle with their nature, never learning to feel at home or at ease in their bodies, and as a consequence never learning to like themselves as they are? What toll did this take of them? How many undeveloped human beings were there because of this repression? Worst of all, relevant because of the revelations of recent years, how many became warped and perverted in their attitudes to sexuality? And all the time we were giving advice and guidance, and in some cases, laying down the law about sex to married people! It was a strange time!

The modern books on human development and on spirituality, which we were all reading in my later seminary years, were fairly dismissive of the traditional way of living celibacy, saying that it stunted growth and led to deep immaturity in important areas of one's life. They talked instead about the need every person has for human intimacy in their lives, not just with people of one's own sex but with the opposite sex also. This was the way towards growth and maturity, the way to become a full human being. My generation of seminarians lapped all this up. Becoming full human beings was the great and ultimate project. Our favourite quotation was the one from St Irenaeus:

The glory of God is the human person fully alive.

We had turned the theology of celibacy on its head and theological and spiritual books began to be written, with high-sounding titles like *The Courage To Be Intimate*, and *The Sexual Celibate*, which supported this way of thinking. We were going to be risk-takers. We weren't going to live the safe but stunted life of isolation. As full human beings we would have intimate friendships with many people of both sexes. We would not be afraid of our emotions nor of entering into the emotions of others. We would also be in tune with the physical, learning to be at ease in the world of physical contact and expressions of physical affection. But we would refrain from 'genital activity'. That now became the no-go area. It was a far cry from the old attitude of keeping your distance from all contact with women. We were excited by this project. Celibacy, far from being a negative, life-destroying experience, now appeared to be opening up as an exciting adventure. We would develop relationships of intimacy with people of the opposite sex, where affection could be expressed physically, but where there would be no genital activity. Neither would there be exclusivity. That was to be the other big sin in our new understanding. Our relationships would have to be in no way possessive. Celibacy meant being available to all, so we could not claim anyone for ourselves alone. That did not seem too big of a problem at the time, since we could have all these exciting and intimate, even if non-genital, relationships.

In our later years in seminary we had many intense debates about this, discussing what would and would not be appropriate for us as celibates. I remember one night being joined in this discussion by an older priest who was a particularly open-minded theologian whom we all admired. He assured us that as long as we could pray together with our woman friend at the end of the evening we would not go too far wrong. That seemed sufficiently loose to give us a lot of scope and we went away happy. I cannot speak too definitely for most of my fellow seminarians, the remnant of us who had survived the long course and the large number of departures, but certainly for me, and I suspect for most of the others, all of this was still largely at the level of theory. The more daring ones, including the ones I had been gooseberry to, had all departed. The types of friendships we had at the time were not just non-genital, but completely non-physical. They consisted mostly of a group of us sitting in little grotty flats with groups of girls up from the country, drinking a few bottles of beer and smoking endless cigarettes, and wondering how we would get back into the seminary without being observed by the superior.

Looking back now I can see that most of what we were reading on this subject was idealistic but naive in the extreme. It originated from the good-natured but soft thinking of celibates who had an awareness of the inadequacies of past attitudes and practices but had little knowledge of the realities of life, and the power and intensity of sexual emotions and passions. The type of intimate, non-sexual relationships that we were encouraged to develop demand a degree of maturity and self-understanding that was totally beyond anything that we were capable of at that time. If one were to set out to try to develop these types of relationships among a group of people, we were probably the last people that would be regarded as suitable for the project. Years of hard experience have now taught me that the modern understanding of how to live the celibate life is infinitely more difficult than the traditional way and has to be lived out in a much more complex world. We are now living through a time of revelation of church 'scandals' in this area. For me what is surprising is not the fact that some have gone off the rails but that most of us have managed to keep some form of stability in our lives.

After my ordination I had an early experience of the difficulty of priestly celibacy, one that the books with their beautiful theories on intimacy had not prepared me for. I learned quickly in my priesthood that a priest, for a variety of reasons, can be attractive to some women. I suppose any public figures who have some skill in communication can appear to be more attractive people than they actually are. And maybe there is an extra attraction that our apparent unavailability gives us.

On one occasion, shortly after my release from the seminary into the unsuspecting world, I was beginning to explore the possibilities of intimacy of this non-sexual kind with a young woman whom I had met on my travels as a missioner. A meal out was followed by a walk on the beach and as we returned to our cars dusk was falling. We had enjoyed a lovely evening together and I felt both relaxed and at ease in her company. In fact I was feeling good about the whole world. Celibacy, which facilitated this type of easy closeness to a lovely woman, wouldn't be too bad after all. As we were saying goodbye standing by her car and thinking of all my training in the need to be able to express physical affection, I offered the young woman a hug and a kiss on the cheek. The ordinary impulses of human nature were more strongly at work in both of us than I had allowed for and before I knew what was happening we were caught in a tight embrace and I found myself being passionately kissed, while also being conscious of her breasts and her hips pressing up closely and urgently against me. Like, I presume, any other heterosexual male, I had often fantasised about what it would be like to hold a woman in a passionate embrace and suddenly it was happening. I knew from her actions and the intensity of the sounds coming from her that she was neither well-versed nor particularly interested in the notion of non-sexual intimacy; if it came to that, and at the rate we were going it would come to it very quickly, she was not one of those who believed that genital activity was a no-go area either.

To use some modern jargon, it was for me a mind-blowing experience; suddenly all my most furtive fantasies could be actualised. Somehow – was it instinct, an innate fear of the consequences or the fact that our heads managed to keep some control over the other reactions of our bodies? – we succeeded in breaking away from each other's embrace and I collapsed into the driver's seat of my own car. I remember gasping for breath, feeling totally disoriented. And I remember, too, the unruly emotions and feeling that were set loose that evening and that came back to haunt me. There were many times during the following weeks and months when I more than half-regretted my control of that evening, my turning away from this wonderful world of passion and desire, this world where I could lose myself in the body of another, even if only for a moment.

Now, almost twenty-five years later, I find myself firmly of the view that compulsory celibacy does not work and that it is in some cases damaging and destructive. Neither do I believe that it is necessary or even helpful for the Church of the future. I am substantially in agreement with Patricia Redlich, when in early 1998 she wrote in a *Sunday Independent* article on the subject:

> With practice, sex can be sent underground. But that is emotionally damaging, since it involves, in a very

real sense, burying ourselves. Sexuality is, after all, an integral part of our whole personality. It's also a dangerous strategy, since unacknowledged sexuality has the unhappy habit of finding devious expression. The real challenge, therefore, for celibate priests, is how to stay in close contact with their sexuality while at the same time never giving it any real expression. That takes great sophistication, great courage and great sensitivity. Particularly for those in pastoral care, faced constantly with the urgency of human need. This task, I feel, is the stuff of saints. But most men are mere mortals.

In my years going around the country, living with priests, I have observed how human and ordinary, and mortal, they actually are. And I have seen the struggles of many of them. I have known some who have managed to live as a celibate in a marvellously rich and free way and have become admirable men of great selflessness and service. They have clearly illustrated the value of celibacy and the contribution it can make to the life of the Church, if it is accepted freely and without any coercion. Undoubtedly not everyone is able to attain this even with the best will and a great degree of prayer. So I have seen all the coping mechanisms at work, men developing into alcoholics, workaholics or people subject to various other types of addiction. I have seen some develop a hard, dismissive attitude towards women and, indeed, towards life in general, while others let out their frustrations in the form of vulgar and suggestive talk, especially over a bottle of whiskey in the company of other clergy. I have seen priests get involved in very furtive and abusive relationships with women, in which there is so much guilt and frustration that they are incapable of showing any tenderness or love. Then they go on a retreat and decide to drop their 'evil' activity, and the woman feels shunned and rejected.

It is a paradox that celibacy can sometimes contribute to sexual irresponsibility in certain people. A priest can easily come to see a purely sexual relationship as being a lesser evil than an emotional involvement. It does not make the same demands and consequently it does not threaten his priestly option to the same extent. It can be instantly given up, and walked away from. Having confessed it and received absolution he can carry on with his life as if nothing had happened. But it must be a strange experience for the woman, who finds the priest so seemingly cold and uncaring as he drops her. Many a woman has tried to confront her clerical ex-lover at this stage, looking for at least some form of emotional response, to be met either with an utter inadequacy and inability to relate to her at that level or a complete denial that anything real ever existed between them. It is a sad situation for both of them. The woman is deeply hurt, and hasn't been helped in any way to bring the affair to an end. The priest has been involved in so much denial inside in himself, denial of his own feelings and of the way he has treated the woman, that he will learn nothing from the experience and may well repeat it in various different forms many times throughout his life. The other classical way for priests to cope with celibacy is to turn in on themselves and become very selfish, surrounding themselves with all types of material comfort as a way of consoling themselves for the absence of human closeness.

There is an alternative though it may still be some time away. I hope I may live to see the day when compulsory celibacy will be a thing of the past and we will revert to the practice of the early Church – and of some of our sister Christian churches. I, for one, will rejoice when it happens.

4

CONFESSION FROM BOTH SIDES OF THE BOX

The hearing of confession used to be a very significant part of the life of a priest. In most cases this is no longer so. The average priest especially in country parishes now hears few if any confessions. There are still a few places, for instance centres of pilgrimage, such as Knock and Lough Derg, and some of the religious churches in big cities, where confession is popular, but in general the practice has greatly declined. Looked at historically, this is nothing to be surprised at. None of the sacraments has gone through so many changes in the way in which it was celebrated as confession. In fact, in the early years of the Church confession was a very rare occurrence. In those days the Christian communities were invariably small groups living in the middle of non-Christian or pagan societies. Their good name was very important to them. So when one of their number did something in public which brought opprobrium on the whole community that person was put outside the group. He or she could return only when a public confession of the sin had been made to the assembled community and the sinner accepted a fairly severe penance as an act of retribution. Private, individual confession was quite slow in developing. It first began to happen in the environs of the monastic settlements, where people started going to particular monks to discuss their problems, to ask for prayer and sometimes to confess their wrongdoing. The monks would assure them of the forgiveness of God. It was the Irish missionaries, who played such a big part in the conversion of Europe to Christianity in the Dark Ages after the collapse of the Roman Empire, who popularised private confession and made it available to the general public. As part of this new development they introduced confession boxes into the churches. It is also interesting to note that for many years confession was heard by monks, who were mostly not ordained priests. It was only around the ninth century that the hearing of confession became the exclusive work of the priest. The style of frequent confession that my generation grew up with is of much more recent origin in the life of the Church. In fact for many centuries the notion of frequent confession was discouraged by the authorities.

Let me say straight away that I have never liked going to confession. In this respect I believe that I am one of many. Nowadays, I go only very occasionally. So when I meet people who as a preamble to their confession tell me that they do not like going to confession either, it always strikes a chord with me. Like all my generation of Irish Catholics I was introduced to it as an obligation, something that had to be done. In a sense that feeling has never totally left me. I realise now that the curate who was in my parish around the time I made my first confession, while he faithfully performed his duty as confessor to his people, had little or no interest in it and possibly didn't even believe very much in it. Long before you had completed telling him your list of sins he had already begun, and was speeding through, the Latin formula of absolution. He didn't seem actually to listen to the sins at all. Maybe it is understandable. I'm sure that the boredom of it all would have been too much for him.

My brother tells a story of himself as a young boy: he was worried about something and he felt that he needed to confess it. In order to be sure it was forgiven he needed to be certain that the priest would give sufficient attention so that he would know that what he was saying had been heard. So his problem was how to get through this impenetrable wall of ritual that surrounded the way the priest heard confessions. He normally sat in the confession box, not facing the penitent, but looking sideways, with his forehead resting on his hand. So my brother began his confession: 'I have something important I want to confess.' He achieved his purpose. The hand came down, and the head turned to look out at him. While he had this amazing degree of attention, my brother blurted out his sin. While he clearly thought it was something of importance, the priest did not. The head went back to its sideways posture, the hand returned to the forehead with a gesture that expressed something like 'Is that all you have to say!' and he was immediately into the absolution.

One of my own unpleasant memories of confession in my childhood comes from when I was about ten years of age. The curate described above had been replaced by another man who was slightly less taciturn but a bit scattered and abstracted. As I prepared for confession on this particular occasion I realised that I had a dreadful sin to confess. I believed I had committed adultery. What offence could I possibly have committed that I was glorifying with the name adultery? I have no idea but I wonder now had it something to do with my experience of sexual abuse. I do clearly remember the anxiety I felt as I tried to work up my courage to confess. There was inevitably a large queue on the day that I decided to face the ordeal. It was a very traditional style of confession box, so that while the priest was enclosed in the box the penitent knelt out in the open and spoke through the grill. I was very conscious of the proximity of the waiting people and my heart was beating madly with the tension that had gradually built up while I waited for my turn to come. Maybe the priest was tired or maybe he was in one of his scattered moods. What he did was to make no comment at all except to give me absolution. It was very unsatisfactory for me. There was a sense of relief in getting it over with but I was left in the same confused state in which I had gone in. And somehow after all the tension and anxiety of the build-up and the sense that I had something really big to tell not even to provoke a comment from him was something of a let-down.

It was inevitable that this style of confession could not last. It survived for as long as it did because of the unquestioning nature of people's attitude to faith in general in those times. Once questions began to be asked about its meaning and purpose, and even though I was not aware of it they were already beginning to be asked by some people as far back as those times, it would undoubtedly be in trouble. It just did not make sense, because it was too ritualised, too divorced from the ordinary reality of life and had ceased to be any type of real human encounter.

In boarding school, in noviciate and through my early

seminary years we were supposed to go to confession every week. In fact the generation before me in my religious congregation was obliged to go twice a week. They could ask for a simple blessing on one of those occasions. They went in to each other's rooms after night prayers, went down on one knee, blessed themselves and said; *'Benedicite, Pater,* for confession.' The priest would then give them a blessing and they would go. It is hard to work out now what was the thinking behind that type of activity but it was the practice of the time.

It must have been a very dull task for the priests who had to come in to ours and similar schools and hear all the students' confessions every Saturday. A priest I know once described this type of task as similar to being pecked to death by ducks! It was inconceivable that you could have something new and worthwhile to say each week. Anyway, it is doubtful if it would be healthy to carry on this kind of analysis of yourself on such a regular basis. For me that weekly confession bore no relation to reality at all. It was purely a ritual. I believed I got something called 'grace' from it and if you asked me what that was I could trot out the catechism definitions of sanctifying and actual grace. In practice it didn't mean anything much. I worked on the vague notion that it was a good thing to do and that like so much of life, things that were good were also unpleasant. I got on with it without thinking too much more about it.

I had a simple way of dealing with sins. I had a list of nine of them. It was my practice to tell three on each occasion, and I know now from years of hearing confession that this was a common practice. Three seemed to be about the right number. Anything less might produce the response:

'Is that all?' And anything more might seem a bit excessive. My list included all the standard ones, which I have since heard millions of times from the other side of the grill: 'I cursed'; 'I told lies'; 'I didn't say my prayers'; 'I didn't do what I was told'; 'I was inattentive at Mass'; 'I was distracted at my prayers'. So these were trotted out, three at a time, in rotation. I might chance 'I had bad thoughts' once in a while but that was a slightly dangerous one, because if you happened to have a particularly zealous priest he could begin to question you on the nature of those thoughts. The main purpose of my strategy was not to provoke any response from the priest but to get the business over with as quickly and as smoothly as possible. In the latter part of my seminary training, when things had become less strict and we were free to make our own decisions, I went through a period of a few years without going to confession at all.

For someone who was, as I have said, no great lover of confession, I ended up as a priest in a religious order whose work in many ways centred around the hearing of confessions. Ironically it has probably been one of the most pleasant and satisfying parts of my life as a priest. I have spent endless hours sitting with people as they talked about the deepest and most intimate areas of their lives and I have discussed and tried to help untangle the most complicated of human situations. It was an extraordinary revelation in the years after my ordination to see how people could be so open and trusting with us. That is why what we call the 'seal' of confession, the obligation not to reveal under any circumstances what a person tells us in confession, is such an important thing for us. Being able to hear a person's confession, when it is a real human encounter and not just going through the motions or performing the ritual, must be one of the greatest privileges in the whole world. For people to trust someone who is often a stranger to them to such an extent that they reveal their deepest selves is very special.

My experience as a confessor hasn't by any means been all positive and I shed no tears over the demise of the practice of frequent confession. Whenever people were not confessing something to do with sex, they fell back on a ritualistic format. It was almost as if, when they had nothing to say about sex, they had nothing to say at all. I have always found it utterly unsatisfactory as a priest to draw that slide and hear a disembodied voice rattle off: 'Bless me Father, for I have sinned. It is six months since my last confession. I cursed, I told lies and I didn't say my prayers. That's all, Father.' In my early years as an enthusiastic confessor I used attempt to open up conversation and try to introduce some type of human encounter into it by saying something like: 'And how are you getting on?' On missions things tend to be different, because a certain degree of relationship has developed over the duration of the mission which would mean that there was a better chance of getting a response but in the ordinary parish situation the question would mostly draw a monosyllabic grunt. I would try again but how many different ways can you ask the same type of question? Something like: 'Is everything going well with you?' By now I would often sense the utter confusion and sometimes even panic of the person on the other side of the grill who probably wondered was he in for an interrogation and concerned what his pals outside were thinking as to why he was so long in the box. So I would give up, deliver a hasty absolution, and let him go. I say 'him' because that type of response was most common from men. Women, given the opportunity, would sometimes settle in to having a chat about their lives. Hearing a series of those type of ritualistic confessions in succession was always, for me, an incredibly boring experience, made more so by my belief that it was also largely meaningless. I would long for someone to come in with some 'decent' sins to tell or with a good story about their lives and a problem they wanted to discuss. That would bring me back to life and I would feel that I was doing something worthwhile again.

I think that there are three main reasons for the enormous change in the practice of confession that I have seen in my life as a priest. Firstly, there has been a decline in the sense of sin, particularly in the area of sexuality, and since in the past people tended to see sin as almost exclusively associated with sex, they naturally have less to tell now and don't have the same sense of urgency about going to confession. Secondly, the fear of mortal sin and of Hell and damnation was much stronger in the past and was being preached with much more vehemence. So people felt the need to go to confession regularly to assure themselves that they were in a state of grace, and ready for Heaven in the event of sudden death. Thirdly, therapy in its various forms has increasingly begun to replace the healing and therapeutic dimensions of the sacrament. There was an interesting internal dynamic that often accompanied the reception of the sacrament of penance in the old days, particularly for adults. The prospect of telling one's sins aroused an intense state of anxiety. The particular sins which caused most fear were usually the ones related to sex and, since even a thought about sex was deemed to be a mortal sin and because sexuality is at the core of our being, most people associate fear of going to confession with guilt about their own sexual nature.

When the penitents made their confession, they expected some comment from the priest, of comfort, encouragement or condemnation. They expected the priest to respond at a feeling level or, more correctly if he did engage with the penitent about the material of a sexual nature that they had confessed, people experienced this as a feeling response. Thus the anxiety gave way to a feeling of relief. As a consequence, confession involved a cycle of anxiety arousal followed by relief. At this level it had some therapeutic value. Today people are generally much less worried about eternal damnation and confession now contains little or no anxiety so it correspondingly contains considerably less relief. People are more likely to find this cycle of response now from individual or group therapy sessions.

What were the stages of change that happened during these years? Up until the late sixties, the traditional style of confession was still prevalent. The sacrament of Penance, or confession, was defined, like the other sacraments as 'the outward sign of inward grace'. It was made up of two distinct entities known as matter and form. The matter was the sins and it was crucial that all sins of a serious nature be told properly, giving the detail of the sins and the number of times they had been committed. The form was the actual telling. For the sacrament to be valid and proper, then, both matter and form had to be correct. Part of the job of the priest was to see that all of this happened. That is why questioning of the penitent was so often a feature of confession in those days. The priest felt obliged to find out as much as he could about the sin so that he would be sure it was validly confessed.

I grew up in the Redemptorists on stories of the long hours spent in confession boxes and of all the mortal sins that were forgiven during a mission. The big achievement of the traditional missioner was to have someone into confession who hadn't been there for many years. And if he or she could be helped to confess a series of mortal sins, then the real purpose of the mission had being achieved. Putting it bluntly, people's souls were being saved. It was a simple, stark theology out of which these missioners operated. If people died in mortal sin they would go to Hell; if they were persuaded to go to confession and tell those sins they had some chance of salvation. Many a missioner came out of the confession box at one o'clock in the day after a long morning of hearing confessions and walked over to his dinner, tired after hours in a confined space, but feeling good in himself as he totted up in his mind the number of people he had saved that very morning from the fires of Hell. That type of belief gave an enormous sense of purpose to the priest's life. He saw himself as constantly in the front line, battling against the Devil for the souls of the people. Is it any wonder that the type of uncertainty that so many of us priests suffer from today was rare in those times?

There are many stories about how long it took people to pluck up the courage to go to confession and the amount of alcohol some had to take in order to overcome their fear. As the mission went on the missioner put great emphasis on encouraging people to come to confession and assuring them of a welcome. Still people were tense and uptight. They wanted to get the ordeal over with as quickly as possible. So they gave out what they had to say in the form of as brief a list as possible. They left anything of substance to the very end, often dropping their voice or saying it quickly: 'I had sex with my girlfriend, Father' in the hope that the priest might not notice and just give them absolution without too much of a lecture. They were generally in a defensive mode, anticipating criticism, and any attempt to open up conversation was presumed to be a prelude to that criticism.

As a consequence, the hearing of confessions on missions in those days, apart from the sense of purpose you got from feeling that you were saving people's souls, was not a very pleasant experience. It was far too much of a ritual, lacking variety and humanity. The people had over the years developed protective mechanisms in the language they used and certain phrases were in common usage which could carry a whole range of meanings. 'Bad actions' could be anything from masturbation to rape; 'company keeping' covered the whole range of courting. And the real dread was for the priest to begin to question the penitent on the precise details of the company keeping. Then you were quickly into the area of 'How far did you go?' In most cases it wasn't that the priests were just interested in the lurid details, though I am sure some were. They were simply trying to make sure that the matter of the confession was stated in the correct form so that the absolution would be valid. 'Bad thoughts' raised the question as to whether or not you indulged or entertained them, or, to use the old phrase, took pleasure in them. Like with so many other difficult aspects of life, the Irish people had a great facility to make jokes about all of this and our folklore is full of confession jokes:

'I had bad thoughts, Father.'

'Did you entertain them, my child?'

'No, Father. They entertained me!'

It was, as humour usually is, a healthy response to what was a particularly unhealthy practice. It was also a defence mechanism against something painful.

A lot of what went on in that era is summed up for me in the advice that one of the older, experienced missioners gave to a young priest who was his companion on a mission and who was just beginning his career in the late sixties. This older missioner was a man of immense experience and reputation who had always been considered an expert in the field of confession and an adviser of the young confessors. On this occasion he was, as usual, taking his role seriously. As they took their after dinner stroll, he began to question the young man: 'How would you deal with someone who was a year away from confession and who confessed that he had committed masturbation once a week for that year?' The young missioner played for time: 'In fact I am meeting situations like that often, and I would be glad of some advice on how to handle it.'

The older man settled happily into his role as mentor, not for a moment doubting the quality or the enduring nature of the advice he was giving: 'I had someone like that myself recently and I said to him: "Would you bet on a horse at fifty-two to one?" He answered me: "No, Father, I would not. Or if I did I would put very little money on him."

'"Well, my good man,' I told him, 'that is all the chance you have of getting to Heaven, fifty-two to one!"' If he died the week of his confession, he would be all right. At any other time of the year he would go straight to Hell, since he would be in a state of mortal sin.'

The clarity, certainty and simplicity of it all is utterly baffling to the modern mind but was accepted not just by the priest but mostly also by the people in those days. That is why confession was such a serious, solemn and frightening business. It was consistently dealing with eternal damnation or salvation. The stakes as they understood them were very high indeed. That old man, who is now long dead, was a good man but it is terrible to think of all the oppression and anxiety that he and those priests who thought like him caused to some people even in this one area. Masturbation is a common practice, especially among men. I would not necessarily agree with those who say nowadays that it is a good and healthy thing to do but to classify it as a mortal sin for each act of which a person would be condemned to Hell for all eternity was nonsense. For some people, it is clearly a compulsive habit, over which they have little or no control. This is especially true for men who are lonely, highly strung or sexually frustrated. The last thing these poor men needed, as they coped with their loneliness and frustration, was to be threatened with damnation.

By the time I was ordained in the early seventies, this style of confession was rapidly losing credibility. Neither priests nor people had any longer the type of black-and-white understanding of life and salvation that sustained it. My training and that of my contemporaries had given us a radically different understanding of the sacrament and as a consequence I don't think we could ever have fitted into that form of confession. I know that I have never been able or never believed it right to question anyone about any aspect of their sexual lives in confession, except in so far as they wished to talk about it themselves. The big difference for my generation of priests was that most of us didn't feel bound by the legalistic observance of the ritual. Things like matter and form were not that important to us. We were trained instead to think more in terms of the spirit of what was happening and to focus on the penitents and what would be helpful for them.

By then a new development had come and I think it is fair to say that it is to the credit of the Redemptorists, who were the great practitioners of the old system, that they recognised the need for change and began to do something about it. The recognition of the need for change coincided with a fairly radical reappraisal of the whole style of mission-giving and the content of the message being preached. An effort was made to redesign confession. The purpose was to get people away from the list of sins and from all the fear and anxiety that went with the practice and help them simply to talk about their lives and in this way to focus on the deeper issues of what was happening in their relationships, family, work, prayer and life.

We began to give sample confessions during missions, showing people how to go about this. It had a radical effect. People took to it with relief and considerable enthusiasm. The whole nature of confession on missions changed almost overnight. People began to come in to talk. It was great for the priests. The boredom was gone and now we found ourselves immersed in the deepest and most complex of human situations. Those were exciting years. Whenever we could we dispensed with the confession box and used sacristies, little alcoves or just sat on benches round the church, and listened for hours as people poured out their problems. We stopped preaching about Hell and damnation, removed all form of threat and encouraged people just to come and talk. The excitement this change generated in the ordinary people was immense. They regularly queued up for hours to speak to us and I can remember staggering out of churches at midnight, dazed and befuddled by the complex and wondrous nature of so much of what I had heard, yet elated by the whole experience.

Counsellors and psychiatrists were few at the time and generally not accessible to the ordinary person, so we were probably the first to come along and invite people to tell us their problems in such a free and non-judgemental way. As a consequence we got the accumulated problems of generations. A box of tissues became now a more important requirement for hearing confessions than the Code of Canon Law. One of the difficulties we faced was that we were not counsellors and most of us had little or no training in this area. My contemporaries and I had done a six-month counselling course and we found it of immense value. Still we were very often out of our depth. I think it is true to say that most of us learned fairly quickly and began to handle the problems we were meeting with at least a degree of sensitivity and skill.

Though we did not realise it at the time, this new approach changed the nature of the whole event and ultimately contributed to the demise of confession as we had known it. It was now no longer a telling of sins, as such, but it took on many of the features of a counselling session. It lost the mystique of the old way. We no longer talked about divine grace and the powerful traditional image of the soul, spotlessly white and free from all stain as a result of the confession, an image which in a sense reached into the mystical, was now never alluded to. Most of all, since we did not talk about mortal sin and damnation, the stakes were not as high. People did not see their salvation depending on what happened in confession. It became, instead, more of a human encounter. People were foraging around in the mundane matter of their daily lives. It was something similar to what happened to the Mass when it was changed from Latin to English and when the priest faced the people and they could see what he was doing.

In recent years our emphasis has changed again and now we often celebrate the sacrament in some communal way. In the late seventies the Church brought out a document allowing for three ways, or rites, of celebrating confession. So we designed a way of going to confession that allows for the telling of sins, but only briefly, to priests who sit or stand around the church rather than in confession boxes. The idea is to put the emphasis on the community dimension of sin and to celebrate the mercy of God. It is a sort of a half-way house between the old system and the granting of general absolution (known in the new document as Rite Three). It can be a lovely ceremony when it is done well and in the right context. And of course it is a far cry from the detailed inventory of a generation or two ago. It did provoke opposition from some of the clergy, who saw it as an effort to introduce general absolution by the back door, and who gave it the derogatory nickname of Rite Two-And-A-Half.

One of the big difficulties in this form of confession is trying to get across the notion of sin having a communal dimension, the notion that my sin affects not just me but the community in which I live, in a culture and Church where sin has always been seen as intensely private and personal, and where it had to do with the salvation of the individual soul.

I am most at home with this form of the sacrament of Penance. It seems to me to be closest to the Gospel idea, where Jesus did not question people about the details of their sins and set no limits or conditions to the giving of forgiveness. It removes to a great degree the power of the priest to question and interrogate the penitent in the sacrament. And some priests have found that hard to cope with. It is understandable, considering their training. I have seen many an older priest, and unfortunately some younger ones too, feeling and looking very uncomfortable as they stood at the top of the aisle giving absolution to a long line of people, with no possibility of interrogating any of them.

On one occasion in the early eighties, when doing this form of confession was still fairly rare, we were conducting a mission in a parish in the south of Ireland, and we suggested to the priests that we would like to have this celebration. The parish priest was nervous and asked me to consult the bishop. The bishop was a nice man but of a legal frame of mind. When I explained what we wished to do I could see he wasn't too happy, but because he was basically well-disposed and wanted to be helpful, he tried to meet me half-way. He said that we could do the ceremony as long as I could guarantee to him that every penitent had the opportunity to tell all their serious sins in number and kind and that every confessor had the opportunity to question the penitent sufficiently to satisfy themselves that they understood the nature of the sin and could make a judgement of its seriousness. I was fascinated by his response. He was speaking a language, and clearly inhabiting a world, that bore little relation to mine. His understanding of what was important in confession was so different to mine. He was concerned about the matter and the form, and having the whole procedure happen correctly, so that it could be classed as valid. My understanding was that our purpose as priests was to be agents for the people of the limitless and unconditional forgiveness of God. It is just one small illustration of the type of struggle that was going on all through the Church at the time in trying to cope with the pace of change.

I have outlined the three stages of confession above as if they were separate and distinct developments. But in reality this is never the case. Even today it is possible to meet aspects of any one of the three of them, depending on where you go to confession and what priest you happen to meet. My image of confession is of an occasion celebrated communally as I have described above. We had invited and inveigled as many priests as we could get for the night, because the crowd was very large. One of the priests, an older man, was clearly much more at home with the traditional format sitting in his confession box and did not approve of what we were doing. He didn't even have to tell me. It was written plainly on his face. As it happened the church was divided into a number of aisles, with barriers between them so that people could not easily cross from one aisle to another. This man took up his position at the top of one of the side aisles. As he stood there, his face expressed his disapproval of it all. When the confessions began the people came out of the seats and queued up to go to whichever priest was nearest to them. Except for this particular aisle. Nobody moved. For twenty minutes we heard the confessions of the rest of the church while he stood there and nobody came near him. That aisle was like an oasis of stagnation in the midst of all the activity. From my vantage point I had a good view of the man and the expression on his face. I did not blame the people for staying put.

Hearing confessions is a great responsibility. People are at their most vulnerable. They have, so to speak, laid themselves bare and can very easily be hurt or damaged. This is partly why I hate the confession boxes so much. Talking to someone through a grill in darkness reduces the communication to the verbal only and even that is conducted through a whisper. The potential for misunderstanding and misinterpretation is endless. An obvious and simple example, which has happened to me a number of times, is where you think you are hearing a young girl's confession and in an effort to be encouraging you say something like: 'You are a great young girl,' to be sharply reprimanded from the other side of the grill: 'I am a boy.' When you are dealing with something very sensitive in a person's life it is so difficult to speak through a grill into darkness or semi-darkness, and misunderstanding can be much more serious. That is why it is much easier to have someone sitting across from you, where it is possible to talk things out and where you can see from the expression on their face how they are responding to you.

I have heard many stories of how people were deeply hurt by what was said to them in confession. I am sure that some of it was due to the ignorance or abrasiveness of the particular priest. I am equally sure that some was caused by the circumstances in which the confession was being heard and the fact that the penitent totally misinterpreted the intentions of the priest. Many confession boxes are not properly soundproof, so they do not provide the necessary privacy. It is a dreadful experience to be hearing confession in such a box, with a queue of people outside. You are trying desperately to keep your own voice and the voice of the penitent down to a whisper, and then someone comes in and says very loudly: 'I'm a bit deaf, Father'. What can you do? In order to say anything you have to raise your voice to such an level that it will be heard clearly by everyone outside. My main effort at a time like that is to do what I can to prevent the person telling any sin at all, but if he or she is old and traditional, as is often the case with a deaf person, that is almost impossible. I was recently hearing in a confession box and when I pulled the slide at one side a woman said to me that the soundproofing was not good and that we could be heard outside. I thanked her and then in the lowest voice possible I proceeded to invite her to make her confession. She proved her point by saying to me: 'Well, my confession is exactly the opposite to the one you have just heard on the other side!'

I have known a number of priests who were unsuitable to the task of hearing confessions but who unfortunately spent their lives doing so. For a priest who has a weakness for power and control over others, confession can be a great outlet. It is the ideal opportunity for lecturing people and telling them how they should live and what they should think. For the priest who tends to be a morally righteous type of person, the tendency is to impose the law on the penitent in a rigid, unbending way. This is very damaging. It can equally be done by the scrupulous priest, who is burdened by the thought that he will have to answer to God on the last day for each confession he has heard. He is not able to be flexible. Unless he asserts the strict letter of the law in each situation he will be worried for himself. This kind of priest makes a dreadful confessor. And of course you have the obsessive person, as you have in all walks of life. A priest who has an obsession with sexuality, as some frustrated celibates can have, will be questioning the penitents about the details of sexual behaviour in order to satisfy his own lurid imagination. Others, not quite so destructive, can be obsessive about some form of devotion or religious practice, and they impose this on their penitents as if it was central to the faith.

The hardest person to deal with always is the scrupulous person. Scrupulosity is not really a religious problem. It is more a nervous condition that expresses itself in this way. It takes the form of a person who has a compulsive need to tell their sins and no matter how often they have told them they do not feel satisfied or forgiven. A person who is a really bad case of scrupulosity can go to confession any number of times, even as often as a few times in the one day and yet not find peace. From a confessor's point of view they are particularly difficult, because their condition is impervious to any form of reasoning. It is a compulsion. If the person is a regular penitent, some relief can be found by giving them a formula for expressing their sorrow in a general sense without going into any details about sins, and by insisting that they stick to it. But the effect of using such a formula is to contain the problem rather than to solve it.

While I say it is not a religious problem as such, it is an interesting fact that it was a very common condition among the older generation but is quite rare among young people today. It is probable that the condition would find a different

103

expression in today's world, and that people suffering from it would go to a psychiatrist rather than to confession.

The frequent confession of just a generation ago is now almost gone. Those who go to confession at all tend to do so once or twice a year at most. A great number of Catholics do not go at all and what those who do go say in confession, what would have been termed in the old days the matter, has changed dramatically. Where a generation ago sex was the main content of confession, now it is hardly mentioned, except by the older people. The young generation, those who still come, will almost never mention anything to do with sex. From being seen as the biggest sin, it is now not considered a sin at all! Yet despite big efforts over the years, justice has never really become the content of confession. How people conduct their business is mostly seen as separate from their religious practice.

I believe that what we have seen happening to this sacrament will in the long term prove fruitful. The practices my generation grew up with had largely lost their meaning. It is my belief that now we need a fallow period, before new and more appropriate forms of confession can be discovered for a new millennium.

The final question I would ask on this topic is this: did the Church use confession as a way of keeping people under control? I think that, particularly in the last few centuries, the answer is that it did. Jesus forgave people's sins without asking any questions or drawing up any conditions. His only words were to say to them: 'Go, and do not sin again'. In the Christian faith we believe that the forgiveness of God is freely given and unconditional. It is there for those who want to receive it. And yet we have managed to hedge it around with so many conditions. You would not be forgiven unless you fulfilled all the regulations and rules about how to partake in the sacrament, unless the matter and the form were both correct. In any organised religion, and very definitely in Christianity, there will always be tension between the laws of the Church and the conscience of the individual. By putting a strong emphasis on confession, on the need to confess each serious sin and on the notion that people will not be forgiven unless their sins are confessed properly, the Church was certainly tilting the balance in favour of law over conscience. As the attitude of the bishop whom I described above shows, the priest was the one who would decide if the conditions were right for the sin to be forgiven. The power was in his hands and he was exercising it. The conscience of the individual and their own unique relationship with God were subservient to that. The sad reality was that for many people, the sacrament of Penance, Reconciliation or Confession, call it what you will, became a symbol of the power of the Church rather than of God's forgiveness.

5

CONTRACEPTION AND THE POWER STRUGGLE IN THE CHURCH

Humanae Vitae, the Papal encyclical on birth control, had already been published a few years before I was ordained. But it was the big issue that dominated Church life, and more specifically confessional practice, during the first ten years or so of my priesthood. Because I was in the seminary and studying theology during those years of the late sixties and early seventies when the theological controversy was at its height, I had the opportunity to become well acquainted with the issues.

Pope John XXIII removed the topic of birth control from discussion at the Vatican Council and instead set up a commission to study it and to act as an advisory body to the Pope to help him make a decision. The commission met for a good number of years and inevitably there were leaks. A general idea of how the discussion was going among the members of the commission began to filter out. It was being strongly suggested that the Church was going to allow for artificial contraception within marriage. Many theologians, even here in Ireland, began to take this for granted and to welcome such change publicly. As a result a sense of expectancy had grown up and many married couples began to use one or other form of birth control. The most prevalent method used was the contraceptive pill, as it could be prescribed on medical grounds, whereas other types of contraceptives were prohibited by state law.

At the time it was interesting to observe how some Irish Catholics resolved their dilemmas of conscience. People could always say that they were using the pill to regulate the menstrual cycle, rather than as a means of preventing conception – something of an Irish solution to an Irish problem! The commission, when it reported, did indeed recommend change but it was not a unanimous recommend-ation. A small number of the members of the commission dissented from the majority report, and recommended instead that the traditional teaching should be upheld. The then Pope, Paul VI, decided to ignore the majority opinion, and instead go with the minority group. So the encyclical came out on 29 July 1968, restating the traditional position, and imposing an absolute ban on the use of any forms of artificial contraception. The Irish hierarchy wheeled out Dr Cremin of Maynooth to face the media and he appeared to take some considerable pleasure in announcing that there would be no change. It was a victory for his side.

Looking back now it was probably a mistake on the part of Paul VI to make a statement on the issue at all. To be fair to him, he had been put on the spot by John XXIII, who was the person who so publicly set up the commission. If nothing had been said the debate would have continued and would gradually have sorted itself out as the consensus of the Church began to work through into practice and the bitter divisions might have been avoided. Instead the making of a statement served to polarise and harden the situation; both sides stopped listening to each other and no form of practical pastoral solution was now possible. The encyclical caused massive shock waves around the Catholic Church and Pope Paul was amazed at the extent and intensity of the negative reaction it provoked. Popes up to that time had not been used to such rebellious reactions to their encyclicals. But the Vatican Council and the general spirit of the sixties had let loose a wave of democracy and free thinking that swept through the Church just as it did the rest of society. A great number of moral theologians were both amazed and outraged. They did not agree and they quickly made it known. The battle had begun and for the next ten years or more it became an issue around which an enormous power struggle developed. I know something, though not a great deal, about the extent of the politicking that went on in Vatican circles both before and after the Pope had made his decision. Theologians like Bernard Haring have written about it. They assert that there was a very deliberate campaign by some within the Vatican to isolate the Pope, and to prevent those of the majority opinion on the commission from having access to him at the crucial time when he was coming to his decision, and that they were very successful in this. Some of the accounts of what went on in the Vatican during this time do not make for very edifying reading.

As regards the document itself I had no difficulty with a lot of its contents. In many ways it is very rich and inspiring. I fully accepted the spirit of it and I saw it as a strong statement of the Christian ideal in this aspect of Christian marriage relationships. I never agreed with the rigid interpretation put on it by the Vatican and reiterated by the official Church here in Ireland. By rigid interpretation I mean those who stated that this teaching had to be imposed on all Catholics, no matter what their situation or circumstance, that held that the use of artificial means of birth control was always morally wrong (indeed some asserted that it was always 'intrinsically evil', whatever that theological phrase, which was bandied around a lot at the time, came to mean to the ordinary person). In saying that I had difficulty with this, I know I was not unusual. Many priests, and the majority of moral theologians, had the same difficulty. In theology I had learned that there was a very important principle for all confessors and spiritual and moral directors. It is what is known as the 'pastoral solution' and it had been accepted as standard pastoral practice for many centuries. Put simply, it stated that a confessor always dealt with penitents on the basis of their individual circumstances and the degree of their ability to cope with them or change them, and tried to get them to do their best in these circumstances, making sure not to impose impossible burdens on them. It was, and continues to be, a most useful principle, which allows a degree of flexibility in interpreting Church law for the individual. The more vocal the opposition to the strict interpretation of *Humanae Vitae* became, the more vehement was the Vatican assertion of its position, and the more it insisted that this was an immutable law that could not be changed or reinterpreted.

Dissent from this encyclical, while widespread and vocal internationally, was very muted in the Irish Church. The most notable and admirable dissenter was Fr James Good of the diocese of Cork and Ross. He spoke out publicly, stating his disagreement with the encyclical. Immediately he came into conflict with the then Bishop of Cork and Ross, Dr Cornelius Lucey, and he was banned from working in the diocese. He moved to Limerick, where he occupied a position in education for a number of years, before going to work on the missions in Africa, where he is to this day. At all times he acted with great dignity and courage and with an enormous sense of loyalty to the Church. He paid a great price in terms of his personal standing and his 'prospects' within the Church, though from what I know of the man I do not think that would have concerned him at all. He was not a man with ambition for higher posts.

In a recent programme on Teilifís na Gaeilge he also expressed regret at the lack of support he got from the moral theologians at the time in Ireland. Some of the better known ones, who knew of the way the wind was blowing in the commission discussions and who expected a positive outcome, were publicly in favour of the use of contraceptives. When the encyclical came out they were shocked. One of them even went underground for a period of time. He returned, totally converted, and became one of the most vehement spokesmen for the official Church line. I remember listening to him speaking one day to a group of confessors and to my amazement he stated that the pastoral solution was no longer an option on this issue. The law must be enforced. There were to be no exceptions. The use of artificial contraceptives was always morally wrong and sinful.

When I began my work as a priest, and indeed for many years afterwards, the issue of birth control was the one that dominated most of our time in confession. I said in an earlier chapter that the Redemptorists had played a significant part in redesigning the practice of confession in the seventies and that it was a significant contribution. The other area where I feel we can take some credit is the fact that we were in the forefront of trying to interpret *Humanae Vitae* in some reasonable way for the ordinary people. We too paid our price. We fought many a hard battle with bishops and priests, and we were banned from a number of dioceses for being 'soft' on birth control!

I think we missioners got much more exposure to the problem than the average priest in a parish. This was because when we arrived in the parish people came to us for a second opinion. The word quickly spread that we were willing to talk about it, that we were often more flexible (or lax, depending on your point of view) than their own priests. This was not always the case. We too had some men who were insistent on laying down the law. I remember going to one parish where the priests told me that they had a Redemptorist mission some years previously, with a particular man on the mission team. In their own words, they said: 'It took twelve months for us to undo the damage he had done.' The problem was that he was part of a team that presented a caring and open image, which lulled people into a false security as far as he was concerned. They came to him with their birth control problems and got a serious telling off! The priests wanted an assurance that none of the team of which I was a part would repeat that performance. It is also true that I came across many diocesan priests who dealt with the issue with great skill and sensitivity.

The result was that I and most of my companions spent endless hours in countless confession boxes listening to married people, almost invariably women, explaining their circumstances to us and asking our opinion. It was an incongruous situation to be in. Here was I, young and inexperienced, having no personal knowledge of marriage or sexual relationships and having a poor understanding of the physical, mental and emotional make-up of women, being asked to make judgements and give advice on the most intimate area of their lives. I heard stories of women who were terrified of getting pregnant for various health reasons and did not want to commit sin by using contraceptives. Another very common situation was of the woman in her middle years, who had got too old to risk pregnancy with any degree of safety and yet was potentially fertile. This situation could go on for up to ten years in a woman's life.

The natural methods of family planning, in particular the Billings method which is the one that was most promoted at the time, have a lot to recommend them, but to assert that they worked well for all women in every situation never made any sense. I could never feel comfortable about telling a couple that they must abstain permanently from sexual relations, which was the other solution being offered by the Church. If they wanted to come to that decision themselves, for whatever reasons, that was their business. I did not think that I had the right, or the understanding of their situation, to impose this solution on them. I also felt that rather than being a solution it could lead to much more serious problems and even to the break-up of the relationship. I considered that the preservation of a good marriage relationship was of far greater moral value than the use or non-use of contraceptives.

After generations of dominance by the Church, people in Ireland had little or no skill in forming their own conscience. They constantly looked for a decision from the confessor on what was right or wrong for them. They wanted to know if it was a sin, because they still thought in terms of mortal sin, and the fear of going to Hell. So they wanted to be told that they could use some form of artificial birth control and not go to Hell. It was a most frustrating position for a priest to be in. If I told a person that the use of some form of contraceptive in their situation would not be a certain cause of damnation, there was a strong probability that some other priest would contradict this at a future confession and refuse to give them absolution until they gave up their 'evil' practice. Or a statement from the Vatican, or the bishops, asserting the official line would throw them into confusion again. So I always, if I could, tried to help them to make the decision for themselves. It was a tortuous process. Trying to explain to people who had never made a decision for themselves in anything to do with religion, how to go about forming their conscience, was so difficult. Doing it in a confession box, as was most often the case, made it even more hazardous. You would think you were doing well and then: 'But is it a sin, Father?'

Sticking to the principle of what I was trying to achieve, I would answer: 'I don't know. That is for you to decide in your situation.' I am sure that many a person left me feeling dissatisfied but I considered I was doing no service to them by becoming their conscience. Gradually the message began to get through, and more and more people slowly took responsibility for their own decisions and stopped confessing it at all.

There is no doubt that some priests abused their position as confessors during these years and became very obtrusive and interfering in the private lives of people. A good friend of mine, a married woman, told me of an experience she had in confession at one of our Marian shrines some time in the mid-eighties, when one would have thought that the issue had begun to die down. She was making a fairly routine confession, because she considered this to be part of the pilgrimage. When she had finished what she described as a little list of fairly innocuous sins, the interrogation began:

'Are you married?'

'Yes, Father.'

'How long are you married?'

'Five years, Father.'

'And how many children have you?'

'One, Father.'

'Only one! And why is that? Are you using some form of birth control?'

At this point my friend was getting very angry, and she told the priest that it was none of his business. She got up and walked out of the confession box. Her initial reaction was to say to herself: 'That finishes me with the Church.'

When she had time to cool down and reflect a bit on what had happened, she realised that it would be foolish of her to allow the behaviour of this priest to come between her and her faith. He had absolutely no right to question her on aspects of her life which she did not choose to bring up herself. And to start lecturing her on how many children she should have was totally outside his competence and his rightful role.

I know that there are many women around the country who could tell similar stories to that one. It was not a glorious era in the life of the Church in Ireland or indeed elsewhere.

A great deal of moral bullying and unpardonable interference in the private lives of people went on. Some priests were taking out their anger at, and disapproval of, those theologians and fellow priests who dissented from the teaching by imposing it more rigorously on the people who were coming to them in confession.

I have the impression that not all priests dealt with the issue in any sort of direct way when they met it in confession. A great many seem to have avoided it. People came to them in confession and confessed that they were using contraceptives. The priest did not make any comment but simply gave them absolution. While I would at this stage in my life be generally in favour of this approach by the confessor to people confessing sins, because it gives the penitent total freedom as to what he or she wishes to bring up, I think that in the particular situation I am discussing, some priests could have been more helpful to people in teasing out with them whether or not they had actually sinned by using contraceptives. In other words, and to use the old concept, was what they had confessed matter for confession at all? The fact that the priest didn't comment or didn't make any effort to discuss the significance of individual conscience in the matter reinforced the belief that using contraceptives was always sinful.

The people had been schooled in the 'firm purpose of amendment' era, which meant that they believed that one's sins were forgiven only if one resolved to stop the sinful behaviour. They knew in their hearts that they were going to continue using contraceptives, because they had decided that was the best option for them in their circumstances. So they began to feel more and more alienated from the sacrament of Penance, went to confession less and less, and many eventually gave up the practice entirely. I think that there is great sadness in the fact that, because of the dilemma in which they found themselves, which I believe was really an unnecessary dilemma brought about by an improper understanding of the issues involved, many people lost touch with a tangible expression of God's forgiveness.

Gradually, over the years, a flexible pastoral practice became the norm, with few exceptions. Even then the official line was still held in public. Occasionally I, and some other preachers, attempted to say something from the pulpit reflecting this more flexible pastoral line but it was fraught with difficulty. I remember in one parish where I gave a talk on the topic during a mission, basically suggesting that there were situations in which it might be permissible to use artificial contraceptives without committing sin. By this time many bishops' conferences around the world had come out with statements about how to deal with the problem in a pastoral way, and they were very helpful. I was using these as my authority. The following day the parish priest, who had not been present at the talk, but to whom it had been reported, was in a state of great alarm. He came to discuss it with me. Like a great many priests, he had not read any of the documents around the issue, so I gave him copies of some of them, and discussed the whole approach with him. Gradually I came to see that he was not able to go with what I was saying. For him it was a deeply personal and serious issue. He believed that as parish priest he would have to answer on the last day for the soul of every one of his parishioners and that if we, whom he had invited into the parish, led any of his people astray and endangered their salvation, he would be eternally responsible for it. Faced with a man who took both himself and his role so seriously, I was overcome by a feeling of hopelessness.

That man was not untypical in not having read anything on the subject, with the exception of *Humanae Vitae* itself. A great deal of material emerged, in particular through the seventies, which was helpful: there were some fairly nuanced statements from the Vatican, documents from various episcopal conferences and volumes of theological opinion. Too many priests are lazy when it comes to study, and it is easier to accept and impose a simplistic version of the official position than to go to the bother of acquainting oneself with the complexities of a question.

On another occasion I remember a parish where the local priests gathered in the sacristy each evening to listen to the sermons given at the mission. One of them, in particular, was inclined to interpret official Church teaching rigidly and dogmatically. On the evening I had chosen to speak on the topic of birth control, I arranged with one of my fellow missioners that when I was getting to that part of the talk, he would generate a discussion on some aspect of the mission with the priests in the sacristy, to distract them from listening! It worked! By that stage we had got so weary of the arguments and of the intransigence of those who held the doctrinaire line that we always tried to avoid drawing them on us. In contrast there was a parish priest of a town in Kerry who took me aside quietly at the beginning of the mission and said to me: 'You might be able to say something about birth control to ease people's minds. It will be easier for you to say it than me. I would get into trouble! Just something simple in your own words, to tell them they are all right.' This man was obviously comfortable with the notion of married people making their own decisions in these very intimate areas of their lives but too frightened to make it known publicly. Again it is a sad comment on the sort of fear that operated at the time.

Some years ago, in an article in *The Irish Times*, Garret FitzGerald summed up a lot of what I have come to believe about the way the Church handled the issue of birth control. In the article he stated that the Church's teaching on contraception had done great damage to its moral credibility. I quote:

> The institutional Church lost virtually all moral credibility with the great majority of people – inside as well as outside the Catholic Church – by its insistence on elevating the issue of the possible impact of contraception on sexual mores to the level of an absolute that must take precedence over all other considerations – including the maintenance of normal relationships by many married couples, and in extreme cases the safety of a wife's life.

This was the crucial aspect. It wasn't, I believe, the teaching itself that was the problem but the fact that the teaching was so vehemently and dogmatically asserted that it overrode the normal pastoral practice of the Church. It was ultimately, as I have said above, a question of power. An immense power struggle developed between those who approved of *Humanae Vitae* and those who disagreed with it. In the struggle the people and their needs were lost sight of. They became, as the common people always do when the powers go to war, the pawns in the battle. I think the debate brought out everything that is bad about the Church as an institution. History will judge us very harshly on this one.

Dr FitzGerald also pointed out another very significant aspect of it:

> Because the vast majority of clergy recognised the moral invalidity of the absolute ban on contraception, and were known by their flock to do so, the disciplinary requirement that the clergy pretend to accept this moral absolutism had forced them to appear hypocritical, thus undermining their credibility in other spheres of moral teaching.

That was, in my view, the worst effect of the whole thing. The Church lost credibility in the moral sphere at precisely the time when the moral fibre of the nation was under greatest threat. Now, when much more serious moral issues are at stake, such as abortion, euthanasia, marital infidelity, the decline of standards in public office and apparently massive corruption in the upper echelons of the financial world, our voice is hardly listened to. During all those years I was working a great deal with young people. It was almost impossible to have any sort of serious discussion with them on morality. They saw the Church as having interest in only one area of morality, i.e. sex, and having only one thing to say on it: *No!* No to everything. People generally say today that the Church lost credibility in recent years because of the scandals. Certainly the scandals have caused problems but the credibility had been lost twenty years ago on the issue of contraception. We showed ourselves to be out of touch with the reality of people's lives, rigid in our imposition of the rules and, ultimately and most damagingly, uncaring.

Why did I stay with it through all those years, when so many of my contemporaries left? In a strange way it was a time when great good could be done by the priest. It was possible to lift enormous burdens from people's shoulders. It was very satisfying to sit with people who had a problem in this area, to discuss it with them at an ordinary human level and help them to see the different issues involved and to assess them in their relative importance. A priest could relieve the minds of people at that level and restore again a normal, healthy, loving sexual relationship in marriages where sex had become so fraught with tension and fear of pregnancy on the one hand and Hell on the other, that the love was in danger of being crushed out entirely. It was great to see a person walking out with the burden lifted from them. The fact that the burden had been put there in the first place by the Church did make it all a bit difficult. Still there was a great sense of purpose and a feeling that some good was being done. I never felt at the time that I was being a rebel or disloyal to the Church in acting the way I did. So much theological opinion, particularly on the Continent and America, was on the side of this type of approach, and the episcopal statements of countries such as Canada and some of the European conferences were a great help. They gave us confidence that we were doing the right thing.

I do look back at that time as a period of serious failure of leadership on the part of the Irish Church. Our bishops held totally to the strictest version of the Vatican line, without any deviation. I know that some of them did not agree with it in private. Because Ireland is small and was at the time overwhelmingly Catholic and because the bishops are generally not too much out of touch with their priests, they must have known of the dreadful traumas that were going on in people's lives over this. It would have taken some courage, though not a great deal, because, as I have said, many other bishop's conferences around the world did so, to make a statement giving some pastoral guidelines on the issue that would have given priests some flexibility in their dealing with the question in confession. It never came; I presume the bishops were deeply divided among themselves. The moral theologians who remained silent must also take some share of the responsibility for the damage done.

Today the use of artificial means of birth control is much less of an issue in Irish life or among Irish Catholics. For someone to mention it in confession now is most unusual. The battle has been fought and won and lost although recently my belief that the issue is no longer a serious one for Irish Catholics was contradicted by a woman theologian I was listening to at a lecture. This woman lives in a very poor area of Dublin city and her view seemed to be that the morality of birth control is still a serious problem for poorer urban women. The middle classes, because they have the education and the access to information to enable them to do so, have come to their own conclusions and gone their own way. The poor, precisely because they don't have easy access to education or information, cannot so readily come to the same decision. If this is the case, then it is a disturbing situation. It is yet another example of how the poor lose out. If the Church, like the state, is economical with the truth about something, the people most left in ignorance are the poor. I think it self-evident that the people who were most liable to suffer through an over-rigid interpretation of *Humanae Vitae* were the women of the poorer classes. Have we to conclude that a Church which is supposed to have a special concern for the poor and the weak is still oppressing them in this area?

The tragedy of the whole bitter controversy, I believe, is that with a bit of common sense and a willingness by the two factions within the Church to listen to each other, it need never have happened. And I am not sure that the lessons have been learned. The way that other issues are being dealt with in the Church today would seem to suggest that they have not: for instance, the difficulties imposed by second relationships where the first partner is still alive, and the reception of the sacraments by people in these relationships; and all the problems around aided human fertility, and especially *in vitro* fertilisation, which is becoming more common by the day. The same attitudes that were shown about birth control are developing in the Church around these issues. A rigid line is being held in public and something very different is happening in private. Nobody in the Church is admitting publicly that this is the case nor are there any official voices publicly encouraging the use of individual conscience. A massive pretence of unity and agreement is being presented. People today are not deceived. All that is needed to clear up the matter and restore some credibility to the Church is an honest and unambiguous explanation of the place that law and conscience play in the moral life, and their relationship to each other. When will we in the Church let go of the desire to control the lives of people and instead encourage in them the facility for freely chosen moral decisions?

Allowing for what I have just been saying, it is fairly clear now that the controversy around *Humanae Vitae* and birth control had some very significant and lasting effects on the Catholic Church both in Ireland and around the world. Thoughtful Catholics began to realise for the first time that the moral teaching of the Church was not an inflexible list of directives that had to be observed in their entirety and without question but that they could begin to exercise their conscience and make their own decisions about what aspects of them applied to the circumstances of their own particular lives. Having explored the issue of authority and conscience in this one area, they began to exercise it in all other aspects of the moral life. From that time on, the traditional power that the Church had held over its people was greatly weakened. Of course, this also coincided with a rapid decline in belief in Hell as it had been presented in the past. The moral sanction that had been powerfully contained in that teaching was now losing its grip.

The other very interesting effect was that the debate and division within the Church resulted in a degree of focus on the theology of marriage and a consequent development of it that had never happened before. The Church fought the battle on the basis that a married couple could use natural methods of regulating conception and in the course of the debate they emphasised more and more the effectiveness of these methods. In doing so they were conceding something crucial, something that Catholic theology had never conceded quite so publicly before, that sexual pleasure without the possibility of conception was permissible and good. In fact a whole theology about the goodness of sexual pleasure in marriage was increasingly emphasised. In conceding this so completely they were actually losing the battle by the very arguments they were using in trying to win it. The more people came to believe and accept that sexual pleasure was a good thing, the more difficult it became to convince them that they should be denied it. This also had a profound effect on priests. They found themselves, by the nature of the debate, forced to become immersed in the new theology of marriage and sexuality. For many this was very unsettling. They had accepted celibacy believing that it was a superior way of life, and that sex was largely sinful and part of the evil nature of the body. The notion that sexual pleasure was good, liberating, life-giving and even holy, as the new theology asserted, made it harder for them to convince themselves that their way of celibate life, with its self-denial and loneliness, was still worthwhile. So I suspect that by trying so hard to hold the line on contraception the Vatican unwittingly undermined the theology that was holding compulsory celibacy together.

6

SOCIAL CHANGE AND MOVING STATUES

Among the many changes I have seen during the span of
my years as a priest, one of the most significant was the
growth of a strong and well-organised traditional wing in
the Catholic Church. This has happened internationally and
in Ireland, and has received great support and encouragement
from the present Pope. While in England it has found a
focus in resistance to the liturgical changes and in the
preservation of the Latin Mass, here in this country it has
mainly focused on two specific areas of life. The first of
these is the long running saga of social legislation that we
have debated and fought over for the past fifteen years. The
second area, in contrast, has been Marian devotion. I will
deal first with my experience of the debates on social
legislation.

Since 1983 we have had in this country two referenda on
issues related to abortion, two referenda on divorce, long
and tortuous debates and various different legislative efforts
about the legalising of contraception and finally a surprisingly
smooth passage of a law allowing for homosexual acts
between consenting adults. These years have been fairly
traumatic ones for the whole of our society and in particular

for the Church, which found it very difficult to discover its appropriate role in the debates. The Church is such an unwieldy organisation with rigid and inefficient methods of government and an enormous weight of tradition, both good and bad, that it finds great difficulty in coping with any sort of change. The change that we have experienced in the last twenty or thirty years wasn't just any sort of change. It was change of an extent and a pace that we never had to deal with before. To use sociological language, you could say that Ireland went from being a traditional to a postmodern society in that time, a degree of change that happened in Britain and the Continent over the period of most of a century.

For priests too it was a difficult time, because to some extent we were in the eye of the storm. There was a widespread assumption for a long time among many ordinary people and also in certain sections of the media that all priests thought the same, that we happily and faithfully parroted the official line, without any ability to have an individual idea of our own. To be a priest meant, in their eyes, that you were little more than an automaton, doing, saying and thinking what you were told. There are certain sections of the media that haven't, even to this day, realised the variety of opinions that are held within the Church and the richness of the tapestry of characters, attitudes and beliefs that go to make it up. For the superficial and lazy type of social commentator, looking for neat pigeonholes to classify people, it is easier to see all of us as like old-style communist apparatchiks, faithfully and blindly implementing the decisions of our superiors.

Not that I should blame the media totally for this, because certain sections within the Church also work on this assumption. There have been major efforts made to present a public show of unity and consent that bear no relation to the reality. This was often done by trying in every way possible to stifle any alternative voices. I have sometimes sat in with a group of priests discussing the particular social issue of the day and have been amazed at the way some assume that you agree with them in whatever line they see as the official and accepted one. I remember on one occasion staying with a priest for the two weeks of a mission in his parish, which was also a small town. He had objected to any type of criticism of the Church and believed strongly that everyone in the media was out to get it. It always surprises me how many priests feel that and how much energy has been wasted in condemnation of the media. I know there is some truth in their view of the media but becoming paranoid about them as a whole is very futile. They are part of modern life and will not go away.

Anyway, each morning at breakfast this priest would look through the daily paper to find the latest attack on the Church and he would read it out for me and invite me to agree with him in his conspiracy theory. For the sake of peace and harmony during my two weeks' stay I went along with him. I hadn't reckoned with the fact that an article I had written some time previously for a religious periodical, commenting on the decline in numbers and quality of applicants for the priesthood and giving some reasons that were not particularly flattering to the Church, would come out at this time and be picked up by the paper. He spotted the headline, and said to me with a somewhat triumphant tone in his voice: 'Listen to this. Here's more of it!' He began to read out the views expressed, not having yet come to the point where they named the source of the views. I, totally unsuspecting, was only half-listening at first until the familiarity of some phrase hit me, and I realised what was happening. Suddenly I lost all taste for my porridge and I realised that I had better, in the words of Willie John McBride, get my retaliation in first. I quickly said: 'I think it is me that is doing the criticising this time.'

'Oh, is it?' he said and I can still remember the way his voice tapered off and how he moved on to another part of the paper. There was a long silence. Though we continued to get on quite well there was a tension between us for the rest of the mission.

The first time we had to vote on a social issue in modern Ireland was the 1983 referendum on putting into the constitution the clause prohibiting abortion. With apologies to the political commentators, I would like to give my version of what happened because it was a very significant event and we are still living with the effects of some of the decisions made at that time.

Abortion was prohibited by law in Ireland and, partly because of our proximity to Britain where abortion was freely available, there was no great public demand for its introduction here. Garret FitzGerald, the Taoiseach at the time, was approached by a group that termed itself 'pro-life', asking that the constitution be amended in such a way that abortion could never be legalised against the wishes of the people. He succumbed to their pressure – with hindsight surely a mistake. Charles Haughey, the leader of the opposition, also supported the idea of amending the constitution. In fairness to both men they were facing a powerful and vociferous lobby group and had they stood up to them they would have run the risk of being branded baby murderers and promoters of abortion. Such was the tone of the debate.

Peter Sutherland was the Attorney-General at the time. He devised a form of wording but it was rejected, both by the lobby calling itself pro-life and by the opposition party. Those were the days before the Tallaght strategy when oppositions tended to see their role as one of opposing in every circumstance. Some government TDs were influenced by the lobby group or maybe they genuinely in conscience could not accept Peter Sutherland's wording. At any rate they didn't support it and the opposition came up with a new formula which was the one that passed through Dáil Éireann and went before the people. Now it was indeed a tangled web. People were divided along party lines and also divided according to their own beliefs. It was a mess.

I was relieved to be away on the polling day and consequently did not have to make a final decision on how to vote. I remember being very uneasy about the whole thing. I was appalled at the way the debate was hijacked by the two extremes and how it quickly became impossible to have any type of reasoned discussion. We have become familiar with that type of scenario since and have to some extent learned to live with the fact that as a nation we are deeply divided on social issues and often have a low level of tolerance for opposing views. Back in those days the extent of the bitterness, division and outright extremism was new to us all and was a very unpleasant discovery. My thinking on the topic was very influenced by the arguments of Peter Sutherland and by the warnings he gave us, which have since proved to be correct, about the ambiguous nature of the proposed wording. His voice unfortunately was lost in the clamour and he was demonised by many. To his credit he has never, to my knowledge, commented publicly on the cases that later proved him right.

At that time the Church was disorganised, lacking coherent leadership and uncertain of its position. It was no longer the dominant voice it had been for so long. Although its power was on the wane it hadn't yet learned to accept the fact that it was now just one of many equal voices in the society. Some of the bishops in particular were still living in the old era of control and domination. Maybe it took the painful experience of those debates for the Church to begin to discover its new role in the new Ireland. The biggest mistake it made was to allow itself to be drawn into the camp of the extreme single-issue group and to be swamped by their line of argument. I think this happened partly by default. The group that was proposing the new wording for the constitution that they intended would forever ban abortion from our shores were well organised and very vocal. They quickly took the moral high ground and the Church, disorganised and confused, was swept along in their wake. Once that happened it had lost the ability to be a reasoned, balanced voice in the debate which, with the learning and talent at its disposal, it could have been. Along with all this the issue of abortion was such an emotive one that many priests allowed their hearts to rule their heads and said and did very foolish things in public, which further served to undermine whatever credibility the Church might have had.

I remember the weekend before the poll. I was conducting a novena in a church in a large town in the south of Ireland. The parish priest was a tall, well-built man, of great learning and culture. We had a long discussion with him on the

Saturday night about the whole issue and I was impressed and fascinated by the extent and degree of his knowledge. He gave us a run down on the whole history of the Church's dealing with abortion and the way that Church and state coexisted on this issue in other countries. I admired him for his knowledge and for the ability that he seemed to show that evening as he talked to us - based presumably on his wide understanding of the issues - to stand back from the heat of the debate and view it objectively and in the light of history. After the best-attended Mass on the Sunday morning I saw the other side of this man and also an example of the sort of conflict we were to become familiar with.

There were some canvassers outside the church on the public road handing out leaflets asking us to vote against the proposal to insert the clause in the constitution. They were fully entitled to be where they were and to be doing what they were doing. They were mostly students. One of them, a young girl of about twenty, small of stature and dressed in the inevitable jeans and sweater, was standing outside the gate leading from the car park on to the road and she was handing a leaflet to the driver of each car as they came out. I could see the parish priest looking at her and feel the emotion rise up inside him and swamp his reason and intellect. His face got red and angry. Then he began to do the most extraordinary thing. In his full canonical robes, red buttons and all, he began to try to stand between the young girl and the cars and to jostle her out of the way. She was much too nimble on her feet and was easily able to get around him. It was a sad and pathetic sight and I often recalled it afterwards. In a way it summed up the confusion and ineptitude of much Church reaction to these issues in the years since. And it was also a good example of how we priests, because of our training or perhaps our lack of it, can be very mature at an intellectual level and at the same time almost retarded emotionally.

As I say, I didn't vote on that particular occasion. I was about a hundred miles away from my polling-station on the day of the vote and working on a very busy schedule, so it would have been difficult. I was glad of the excuse. If I had to make the choice, I think I would have voted against the proposal on the advice of Peter Sutherland. I would have been uncomfortable doing that too, because it would have put me in the same camp as a group of vehement pro-abortion people who, it seemed to me, showed themselves up in the debate to be arrogant and dictatorial in their attitudes. If I voted for the proposal I would equally find myself with some very uncomfortable bedfellows, such as the lobby group that proposed the referendum in the first place. I would have wished for some way to express in the ballot box my abhorrence of both sides.

Is it inevitable that, on issues like this, reasoned debate becomes the first casualty? I regretted afterwards that I hadn't made the effort to vote. In an important sense all these votes that we have had on social issues over the past fifteen years, painful and all as they were, were a defining time in Irish life, and it was important to be a part of the decision and not to leave it to others. As I see it, the result of that particular vote, while mirroring the divisions in Irish society, also served to deepen them. The 'pro-life' lobby group had a resounding victory but as the votes were counted it became clear that they had much less support in the greater Dublin area than elsewhere. This began to be interpreted as an urban-rural divide. It led to a certain anti-Dublin, anti-media prejudice among a fair number of the clergy and the more traditional section of Catholics which survives to this day and has not been helpful.

On the two occasions we were asked to vote on the issue of legalising divorce, I voted 'yes'. I did this for a variety of reasons. I recognised from a long time back that the introduction of civil divorce was inevitable and that there wasn't much point in wasting energy on it. Ireland was no longer a homogeneous society. In fact it was becoming a very complex society, with a great variety of different and deeply held views on most of the important questions. What we had to do in the future was to learn to live in tolerance of each other. Church and state were becoming more separate and I welcomed this development. I felt that the Church would ultimately be in a much stronger moral position when it had no power, when it could no longer have a direct influence on the laws of the state. Then it could speak with the only type of authority it should ever have, an authority based on the truth of what it was asserting. I have always admired the Catholic Church in England for that. It has its own problems but it carries a moral weight and authority in the society far in excess of its numbers. It has earned this position through a consistent statement of Christian values, while at the same time showing itself respectful of the views of others and happy to live in a society at peace with people of different beliefs – and none. It has also been blessed in recent years with a leader of the highest quality in Basil Hume. In contrast, the leadership in the Church in this country has been weak, and weak leadership is more likely to cling on to power and control in order to bolster up its own weakness. The more it does this and the more its authority depends on power and control, the less real respect its voice has. So I believed that the defeat of the Church's position on the divorce question would be in the best long-term interests of the Church.

The Church had another difficulty in this debate. It was dissolving marriages itself and remarrying people in the Church, through the process of annulment, and in this it was flouting existing state law. I know that the Church makes a clear distinction between annulment and divorce. It asserts that in the case of an annulment the marriage had never really existed so that it is not really dissolving a marriage as such. While that type of distinction makes sense in theological circles, it is not so easy or clear to the average person. The practice tended to weaken the Church's anti-divorce position in the eyes of the people.

Deciding how to vote was not easy. Once again I was very uncomfortable with the quality of the debate and I found myself being influenced by the arguments being put by both sides in the opposite way to what they intended. Often when I heard one side arguing for my vote I found myself saying that I couldn't agree with them and I would vote the other way. Then hearing the other side drove me back again. I wonder if there were many others who felt like me? I know that when the last vote, the one that eventually legalised divorce by a narrow majority, was taking place, I was again away from home. This time I drove back to vote. One of the men who was working with me came along but he couldn't decide which way to vote, he was so repelled by the arguments of both sides. In the end he went up to the polling booth, took his ballot paper, folded it and put it in the box.

Even though it would be registered as a spoiled vote, my understanding of the statement he was making was: 'A plague on both your houses.' I could sympathise greatly with his position and I admired his civic-mindedness in doing a round trip of one hundred-and-twenty miles in order to make that statement, even though he knew it would not be clearly heard.

The Church has suffered greatly by allowing itself to be hijacked by lobby groups that have grown up around the issues of abortion and divorce. I am not suggesting that these groups have not got a right to exist and to campaign, but the type of exclusiveness, intolerance of differing views and general moral righteousness that has become part and parcel of some of them is contrary to what the Church should stand for. The idea put across by some traditionalists groups that the Church is a club and that only those who fully ascribe to *their* interpretation of all its teachings can be members of that club, I have always found repugnant. I could never belong to a Church that was a club or any type of exclusive body. I am never comfortable with anyone who sees themselves as being more Catholic than others or better living and morally superior to others. For me the Catholic Church is always a community that has its door open to any type of person who wants to come in. Its great strength is that it can embrace totally different sections of society, the rich and the poor, intellectual and non-intellectual, people of radically different ideas. And most of all it is a great Church for sinners.

The life of a priest is a fairly public one and reactions of all types are inevitable. Over the years, whenever I have taken public stands on social or moral issues, either on the pulpit or in writing, by far the most virulent response has come from the people who are the most self-righteous. Vicious anonymous letters and phone calls are a stock-in-trade of some of them. It is a very unfortunate attitude, which only serves to discredit their cause.

Over the years, as a priest, I have often found myself being abused by both sides. On the one hand the ones who would class themselves as liberals, especially in the media, would make massive assumptions about a person like me and about the views that they would presume I held because I was a priest, would dismiss me as being out of date and out of touch, and the enemy of modern Ireland. In doing that, of course, they show themselves up to be anything but the liberals that they like to portray themselves to be. At the same time the traditionalists would equally abuse me for what they saw as lack of loyalty to the Church and for promoting permissiveness and immorality. The first group would wish to get rid of me from society, while the second group would want me out of the Church. Is it any surprise that I do not have much respect for either group at this stage?

The second aspect of the life of the Church where traditionalist views have crystallised and found a home is in the area of Marian devotion. This is a somewhat surprising and unlikely development, but it has happened. One of the strong distinguishing features of Catholicism, in contrast to most of the other Christian denominations, is the emphasis we give to Our Lady. Devotion to her is a significant part of Catholic life and the Redemptorists have played their part in that. We promote devotion to Mary under the title of The Mother of Perpetual Help. The reason for this is that a famous icon, dating back many centuries and with that title, was given to us by Pope Pius IX in the last century, with the request that we do what we can to make Mary known using this picture and title. So, wherever we are around the world, we conduct novenas to Our Lady, some of which draw enormous crowds of people.

During my years as a priest I have worked on many of these novenas. They are normally very pleasant events; we usually pick a big centre with a large church in which to conduct the exercises and put on a series of sessions each day. We advertise it extensively in advance and people tend to come from a wide radius and attend every day for the nine days of the novena. It generates great atmosphere and excitement, and can also be a very prayerful event. For a preacher it is particularly satisfying. To stand up, for instance, in Galway Cathedral or in our own churches in Limerick or Belfast and to look down and see the place black with people is a great experience. The difference between the novena and Sunday Mass is startling. People come to a novena, as they do to a mission, with the intention of listening, so the quality of attention to what you are saying is much greater. Neither will they complain if the session goes on for up to an hour and they will join in the singing to their heart's content. The novena seems to avoid the type of negative attitudes that so often cling to attendance at Sunday Mass in this country, the desire to have it over as quickly as possible and to be involved as little as possible in it.

In the Ireland of today, where there is a tendency in certain circles to denigrate religion and to scoff a bit at religious practice, the success of these novenas is a source of contradiction to many of the movers and shakers in the society. They work on the assumption that the Church is dead, or at least in its last throes, and they cannot understand why thousands of people still flock to these events. They tend to dismiss them as the last relics of the old superstition. That is one way of interpreting novenas but I suspect that it is wrong. The presence of so many young people at them, often those who never go near a Sunday Mass, would suggest differently. There is an innate human need for something to believe in and some place to turn to in the face of the hardship of life. So much of what passes for modern in this country, in terms of attitude and belief, is fairly shallow and superficial, and does not have anything to say about the really fundamental realities which we all have to face and try to make sense of; things such as birth, life and death. The sort of materialistic attitudes that are becoming common in Ireland today are very individualistic and have a strong tendency towards self-centredness, and are in stark contrast to the idealism that is at the core of Christianity. A belief system that does not point people towards the transcendent has nothing of real importance to say to humanity. And the type of mishmash of ideas that has tended to replace Christianity at certain levels of Irish life has clearly nothing of the transcendent about it.

I have done my bit for devotion to Our Lady in my time but I have always been conscious that novenas have a negative side to them. They play strongly on the emotions which, though not negative in itself, is something that needs to be handled with caution and not exploited. With the custom we have at novenas of reading out people's prayers and petitions and praying for them in public, there is a danger that we will manipulate vulnerable and suffering people into believing that going to the novena is the sure way of having all their problems solved. We could end up presenting a very false notion of prayer and God. With the wrong use of the prayers of petition we could present God as someone whose mind can be changed and turned. We could miss the fact that prayer is really about an awareness that God is always with us, even though the circumstances of our lives may not change.

I remember once during a big novena a number of people had gone missing in a boat at sea. Prayers were said for them at each session over two days and a sense of expectancy built up that they would be found. Then at a large evening session while the priest was preaching his sermon, one of the stewards dramatically walked up the church waving a piece of paper and handed it to the priest on the pulpit. He looked at it and solemnly announced: 'Our prayers have been heard; the men are found safe and well.' The church burst into rapturous applause. Mary had intervened, and the men had been saved. I felt very uncomfortable. I thought we were bordering on superstition and manipulating the emotions of the people. This is a relatively easy thing to do in certain aspects of religious practice but it is a dangerous and possibly destructive practice. Anything to do with healing or miraculous intervention of any sort needs to be very carefully handled, especially with large crowds. False expectations can be created and in the emotion of the moment, people can believe that things are happening which have no basis in fact. Also, at times like these we were close enough to turning Mary into an equal of God, something which some of the modern feminists would thoroughly approve of, but which doesn't have a basis in the Scriptures. I have always felt that in order to counteract the dangers of a novena it was crucial that the preaching at these events would be of the best quality possible, with plenty of sound theology and Scripture, and a minimum of religiosity. And I am happy that in general the novenas we conduct conform to this, and have helped to move the people forward rather than backwards.

Some of the things that have happened around devotion to Our Lady in the last twenty years have been strange in the extreme. I am referring to the outbreak of alleged occurrences of moving statues, apparitions and messages. This is an international phenomenon but we have had more than our share of it in this country. The first real instance was at the grotto in Ballinspittle, a small village in Cork. Before we too easily dismiss this now, let me point out that it was taken very seriously at the time. The papers were full of it, and even sceptics like Conor Cruise O'Brien went down to investigate and report on the phenomenon! When it was at its height I was giving a mission in Cobh. There were a few of us, and we were visiting all the homes in the parish. Almost every house we went into we were asked the same question. 'What do you think of Ballinspittle?' None of us had been there. So one night close to midnight we sat into a car and drove over. There must have been about three hundred people gathered at the wayside grotto. A makeshift pole had been erected with a floodlight on top of it. The statue had the usual circle of lights in the shape of a halo around the head. The people were saying the rosary and singing hymns to Mary. We mingled with the crowds. People were gazing up at the statue. Because of the circle of light around it the face was in darkness. Every now and again someone would burst out: 'I see it moving! Look!' or 'I see the face of Padre Pio!' Other people were seeing the Sacred Heart or some of the saints. I remember a very uneasy feeling coming over me. I was in the presence of something I did not fully understand – and that is always uncomfortable – but I was sure that what was happening there had little or nothing to do with religion. The statue was not moving and no supernatural figure was appearing there. Of that I was certain. What I was unsure of was what was drawing the people there and what they were searching for.

The reactions at the time were many and varied. There is no doubt that some people, myself included, regarded it as superstition gone mad and felt that it was making a laughing stock of the Church and of religious belief. Others saw it as a sign that the end of the world was near. Some said it was an indication of how corrupt and sinful we had all become and that God could no longer have patience with us. This was a last warning. Happily the innate sense of humour of the Irish also had a field day. Numerous jokes about moving statues were being told. There were cases where statues were taken off their plinths and hidden away, and replaced by a notice saying something like: 'Gone to tea,' or 'Back in an hour.'

The Church said little or nothing at an official level at first but it was much debated. The most commonly held view was that in itself it could be regarded as a fairly harmless, if eccentric, activity. People gathering at a grotto to pray and sing hymns cannot be doing any harm, it was said. And isn't prayer good, wherever or however it is happening? I was always impatient with this view. The act of saying prayers does not in itself make what is spurious and false into something good. As time went on a number of bishops took very clear and definite stands against particular manifest-ations in their own dioceses, and they are to be praised for doing so. I also remember the statement of a Dublin parish priest at Mass one Sunday morning during that summer when the events at Ballinspittle were at their height. He said to the people: 'If you are going to west Cork this summer on your holidays, I would ask that you honour Our Lady by staying away from Ballinspittle.'

The next few years saw a surge of this type of event which is still continuing, though not with the same intensity. Large crowds can still be guaranteed to gather if there are reports of an apparition taking place. Just a few months ago two-and-a-half thousand people gathered at a roadside statue of Our Lady in County Tipperary that was reputed to be moving.

There is another aspect of this phenomenon which has become almost an essential part of it in recent times and which is considerably more dangerous. I am referring to the fact that, as time goes on, these apparitions are being associated with messages from Our Lady for the world. There are now books of these messages freely circulating. As one old nun said to me recently: 'For a woman who is almost silent in the Scriptures, she has got a great burst of talk in the last few years!' This has added a new dimension to the events, which is a bit more problematic. We had all heard about the messages of Fatima and particularly the third 'secret', which was reputed to have dire warnings for the world; so much so that the Pope, the only one who could read it, was so upset by it that he decided not to reveal it at all. Medjugorje made such messages popular and indeed respectable. Now lots of people are claiming individual apparitions and messages. They are getting more and more extreme and bizarre as time passes. For instance, once after giving a mission in the parish of Cappoquin, where the Melleray grotto is situated, I got a letter from one of the people associated with the grotto to tell me that Mary was very displeased with us, the missioners, because we did not sing her favourite hymn, which is, the letter said, 'I'll Sing a Hymn to Mary'.

Sociologists and historians tell us that these sorts of phenomena happen at times of great social change and upheaval, and are perfectly understandable. They express people's need for certainty and security. That is fair enough, and we are certainly in a time of social upheaval, when so much of what people held dear and based their lives on is being challenged and swept away. I have no difficulty with that, and if people find comfort in these manifestations, well and good. They should not, however, be allowed to get mixed up with religious faith, because they ultimately bring it into disrepute. The Church has tended to stand on the fence to too great an extent when these things occur, although there have been some honourable exceptions. Of course the way that the Church has approved of and promoted Lourdes, Fatima and Knock, and the use it has made of the reported 'three secrets' of Fatima, has put it into somewhat of an ambivalent position. In the early days of Medjugorje a great number of Irish priests and religious flocked there, and lent it considerable credence by their presence.

Is Our Lady appearing or has she ever appeared? If you answer yes to this, how do you begin to distinguish between those that are genuine apparitions and those that are not? Much more important is the second question. Is she, when and if she appears, giving messages for humanity? If the Church believes that to be true, or even likely to be true, and equally if you or I as individuals believe it to be true, then it becomes a matter of considerable seriousness. Mary, we believe, is the Mother of Christ, who is God, and she is in Heaven, body and soul. That is all part of our faith. If she is genuinely appearing, then what she is saying must be presumed to be direct messages from God and that is of great significance. Our faith is based on the Bible, which we believe to be the Word of God but it is two thousand years old and more and the difficulties of language, culture and time make it hard enough to understand clearly or with certainty. A message coming directly from Heaven to us today would surely supersede it.

Of course none of the Church authorities treat the messages from any of the Marian shrines with anything like that degree of seriousness. This leads me to believe that nobody at any official level in the Church nor any expert in theology actually believes any of this. Yet mostly they do not say so publicly. They tend to play along and, in a sort of patronising way, allow the people to indulge their fantasies. Maybe this is the right way to deal with this type of phenomenon – the Church has great experience in these matters. The problem is that in our time the whole thing is getting more and more extreme and the content of the supposed messages more wild. Mary is being increasingly presented as some sort of apocalyptic messenger, with dire predictions of doom and destruction for humanity.

When I was young, God was seen as a distant figure, prone to anger and quick to condemn. We have slowly succeeded in changing that picture and have rediscovered the closeness and care of God for us. Now some of the old attitudes are resurfacing and being put into the mouth of Mary. Appropriately enough she is, if we can judge by the messages, undoubtedly a traditionalist. I have yet to hear of any message that has anything positive to say about the Vatican Council or any of the changes that have happened since then. She has increasingly been used by the traditionalists in their campaign against every change. I feel this is a sad development, and it is time that the Church once again reclaimed Mary and gave her the rightful place which she commands in the Christian story. I think that a stand will eventually have to be taken and the Church will have more clearly to distance itself from all reports of Marian apparitions.

In this chapter I have been describing the growth of a strong traditionalist wing in the Church and pointing out some of its inherent dangers. In itself it is not surprising that such a large organisation as the Church would contain a great variety of views. Using the terms 'liberal' and 'conservative' is one way to describe the different viewpoints in the Church. These are very inadequate categorisations, which fall far short of describing the complexity of beliefs and values that are part of today's Irish Catholic Church. What we can say is that there are people within the Church who hold different, often opposing, views and hold them very strongly. For how much longer will it be possible for the Church to contain all of us with any degree of unity? This inclusiveness will only be possible if we can show a great deal of tolerance towards each other. That is why the intolerance of much of traditionalist opinion disturbs me. I regard it as the biggest threat facing the Church today.

7

THE MASS: SACRED SACRIFICE
OR ROUTINE RITUAL?

Most of us priests remember our first Mass and I have described some aspects of mine in the opening chapter. The first Mass was always considered a highlight, in some ways even overshadowing the ordination of the previous day. The way in which the event is celebrated has changed greatly since my day. Nowadays it very often tends to be similar to the marriage celebration, built around a big, formal meal in a hotel. I am not sure that this is an appropriate way of celebrating it, particularly when it borrows many of the more commercial and even vulgar aspects of the marriage celebration. I have been at dinners after first Masses at which the cake was cut by the young priest to the flashing of many cameras, telegrams were read, the speeches bore an uncanny resemblance to those of the wedding meal and even painful off-colour jokes were told. Since the whole notion of priesthood had its origins in the idea of a Christian community and the need for someone to lead that community in its celebration of the Eucharist, I think that a priest's first Mass should be a community event. Any celebration that may take place after it should be simple and involve the whole community.

The celebration of Mass has for many centuries been considered the high point of a priest's life, the *raison d'être* of his ordination and his existence. This way of looking at the function of a priest came out of a very particular understanding both of Eucharist and of priesthood which bears little resemblance to the origin of both in the early Church. The Eucharist originally was the meal or 'table fellowship' of the community, with one person appointed and ordained to be president or leader of the celebration. It was a re-enactment of the Last Supper, where Jesus sat at the table with his apostles and ate a meal with them. Even as early as the first letter of St Paul to the Corinthians we can see that abuses began to creep into the celebration:

But in the following instructions I do not commend you, because when you come together it is not for the better but for the worse. For, in the first place, when you assemble as a church, I hear that there are divisions among you . . . When you meet together it is not the Lord's supper that you eat. For in eating, each one goes ahead with his own meal and one is hungry and another is drunk.

The frailty of human nature was already asserting itself and the celebration of the Eucharist was becoming corrupted. Instead of being the high point of the community fellowship, it seemed, apparently, on occasions to become a vulgar display of wealth and gluttony, from which some were excluded.

The Church is a great organisation for making laws and the Code of Canon Law is a large book. Whenever any problem arises the response of the Church has been to make a law to regulate it. That is the way it has always dealt with difficulties: draw up laws and regulations to keep the situation under control. As the Church became bigger and more powerful, its legislation grew in volume and detail. This applied to the Mass probably more than to any other aspect of Church life. By the middle of this century the amount of legislation covering the correct celebration of Mass by the priest was enormous, and the study of rubrics, as the laws to do with the celebration of the Mass were called, was a major part of seminary training. Not only did the priest have to observe these rubrics while saying Mass but their observance was imposed under pain of serious, and in most cases mortal sin. There was no activity that a priest could engage in where it was potentially possible to commit so many mortal sins in such a short period of time as in saying Mass.

This caused dreadful problems for any priest who had a tendency to scruples, as a good number have always had. I remember some of these when I was a student. It was pathetic to watch them as they tried painfully to get through the Mass each morning without committing sin. The words of consecration, in particular, caused them most difficulty. The law said that each of the words of consecration had to be enunciated clearly, distinctly and in its entirety or else the Mass would not be properly celebrated and a mortal sin would be committed. The relevant words of the first part of the consecration of the old Latin Mass were: '*Hoc est enim corpus meum.*' If you were serving their Mass (one of the less pleasant tasks of the student during my seminary years) you would kneel behind one of these scrupulous priests, trying to contain your screams of frustration, as they laboured: '*Hoc . . . h-h-hoc . . . h-h-h-hoc-c-c . . . h-h-h-hoc-c es-s-s-t-t . . .*

It could go on for anything up to five minutes, with the sounds emanating from the priest resembling someone who was being strangled, as they tried to ensure that they said each word fully and correctly. And then the consecration of the wine had yet to come, with its much longer formula: *H-h-h-h-ic-c-c-c . . . e-es-s-t-t e-en-n-n-im-m-m c-c-c-calix . . . (Hic est enim calix sanguinis mei . . .)* and on it went. It was dreadful.

This painful performance at a side altar in a chapel at seven o'clock in the morning, which wasn't particularly strange or unusual at the time but in retrospect appears almost bizarre, was very far removed from the early Church celebration of the Eucharist. And I can't help contrasting it with the free spirit of a priest friend of mine, who sometimes tended towards absent-mindedness. Especially on weekdays he would wander through Mass with his small group of parishioners without any great concern either for rubrics or exactness. One morning, having reached the communion part of the Mass, he paused, looked down at the people in a daze, and said: 'Did we have the Consecration?' Neither he nor they were too worried. They were very fond of him, because he was a warm, affectionate person and whatever way he celebrated the Mass was good enough for them.

Another story from our Redemptorist tradition encapsulates the two contrasting attitudes to ritual and rubrics. A man was celebrating his golden jubilee of priesthood in one of our communities. As is normal in such situations there was a jubilee Mass, with the jubilarian as principal celebrant. He was so hyped-up about what he was going to say to the community in his homily that he forgot to read the Gospel, and launched straight into his talk. The Mass continued but one of the other priests, burdened down with scruples, got more and more uneasy. Would the Mass be valid if the Gospel had not been read? By communion time he had worked himself into a state of alarm and when communion was over and everyone was sitting in quiet for a moment, he went to the celebrant to remind him that he had not read the Gospel. The celebrant, high on the occasion and what he regarded as the marvellous talk he had given, was not pleased by this display of rubrical exactitude. He stood up angrily, walked over to the lectionary on the ambo and in a low voice but very distinctly was heard to say, 'The fuckin' begrudgers!' followed by, 'The Lord be with you', as he read the Gospel.

In the monastery during my student years each priest celebrated Mass before breakfast. Since only one priest celebrated the common Mass, all the others said their Masses at a side altar. There could be anything up to ten or twelve Masses going on at the same time in the same church or chapel, each an intensely private act. Each priest was doing what he was ordained to do, saying his Mass, without reference to the other priests (saying theirs) or to the congregation, who were relegated to audience status and a totally non-participatory audience at that. What I believe to be the essence of the Mass, the community celebration, became completely absent from the process. It had become the property of the individual priest. To emphasise this he had even turned his back on the people as he said it. He used Latin, which was not just a foreign but also a dead language that they could not understand. From being a group of people sitting around a table sharing a meal, the Mass had gradually come to consist of a priest on an altar surrounded by rails to keep the people out, with his back turned performing his ritual. No wonder it more and more assumed magical proportions in the eyes of the faithful.

At the time most people, myself included, saw nothing wrong with the use of Latin. Now, however, we all have a better understanding of the fact that having a specialist language is an important aspect of professionalisation. As professionals want to close ranks, to corner the market in their own area of expertise, to build up their status, they create a language that can be understood only by their own colleagues. (In the past only the Church used the term 'laity'. Now all professions talk about the 'lay person' as the person who does not have their knowledge.) Even though Latin had its own charm and lent a special mystique to Church ceremonies – and there are still some people who go out of their way to attend the occasional one that is said – it added greatly to the perceived power of the priest and to the exclusion of ordinary church members.

There was undoubtedly an element of mystery contained in the way the Mass was celebrated. The fact that the actions of the priest, up on the altar and facing the wall, were largely hidden from the people and that the language was in-comprehensible, made it easier to believe that something very profound was taking place. It was easy to believe that this reality belonged to another world. It was the symbol of a remote God who manifested his deity in a quasi-ethereal manner while we looked on. No one spoke of being bored, because there was no question of having any active part, or of being entertained. It is probably true to say that there was then, and continues to be, an inadequate understanding of the nature of the Mass, either of its re-enactment of

Christ's single sacrifice of himself to the Father in which the world was redeemed or of the Mass as a Eucharistic meal.

When the changes came we went rapidly from the transcendental to the practical. The priest faced us, he spoke our language, we saw and heard what went on at the consecration. It became accessible to us; what was extraordinary became ordinary. We were no longer observing something outside of ourselves and our world. It was here that the lack of a basic theological understanding of the Mass became crucial. Without that, and with the mystery taken away, it lost its power to lure us. People began to complain, to say it was boring and the priest, who seemed awesome as he spoke Latin, became someone whose diction, voice and accent were criticised. Now that we can see the bread and wine, see the actions being performed and understand the words being spoken, it is much harder to believe that a real transformation takes place during the Mass. Consequently belief in what we call transubstantiation, the changing of the bread and wine into the body and blood of Christ, is not as firm as it used to be. I believe that part of the difficulty that surrounds the Mass today, and the decline in attendance at Mass in recent years, are caused as much by how the Mass was perceived in the past as by anything that is happening now.

The priest gets a stipend – money – for saying his Mass. The original notion of the stipend was as a contribution to his upkeep. It was only later that it became linked to the celebration of a particular Mass. It is a pity that this happened. The folklore of traditional clerical life, and indeed Catholic life generally, is full of stories of ghostly priests coming back from the dead to request that the Masses they had either neglected to say or had not said properly should be said for them. My uncle, who was a great storyteller and loved to embellish his tales, used to tell a story of a haunted house in the midlands of England. In his young days he travelled much around England, picking up work on the building sites wherever he could and staying in any lodging house that would take him. Having arrived in a particular village and, discovering that there was work available, he went to the local pub and, after a few pints, began inquiring if there was accommodation available. The landlady said that she had a room but that any other person she had put into it had always left in a hurry in the middle of the night. Fortified by the alcohol and by the fact that he had fought the Black and Tans, and believing that he could handle anything that the English could throw at him, even their ghosts, he accepted the room. During the night he was woken from sleep by the bedroom door opening and a coffin came gliding in, suspended about three feet from the ground. It came over parallel to the bed, the lid slowly opened and the occupant, a man, sat up. My uncle, now wide awake and also sitting up, addressed the man in the most civil west of Ireland fashion: 'How're you doin'?'

The man in the coffin answered, equally civil: 'Not too bad. And how's yourself?'

'Is there something troubling you?' asked my uncle.

'Yes,' the man in the coffin answered. He then went on to explain that he was a priest, that there was one Mass he had been asked to say and had received a stipend for, which he had not said, and as a consequence he could not rest in peace.

'Would you have that Mass said for me?' he requested. My uncle assured him that he would be happy to do so. Then he paused for a moment and, ever practical, he said to the man in the coffin: 'You wouldn't by any chance have the price of the Mass, would you?' The ghostly face fell and the spirit tapped the two sides of the garment he was wearing. 'I'm afraid there are no pockets in the shroud,' he said sadly.

'Ah, don't worry', said my uncle. 'I'll look after it.' Then the man lay back, the lid slowly closed and the coffin glided out the door, never to appear again.

'The price of the Mass.' That is how the stipend has come to be seen. Some efforts have been made in recent years in certain places to separate the notion of money from a particular Mass but I am not sure how successful they are. One of the difficulties is the practice of giving Mass cards at funerals, which has become very common. This has been responsible to some degree for trivialising the Mass. In the proper understanding of the Mass it makes no sense to pigeonhole it in this way. As I have said above, the Mass is the re-enactment of Christ's great act of redemption of the whole world. To assign a Mass to any particular individual, alive or dead, and to say that it is celebrated for this person alone makes no sense at all. Most priests are well aware of all this but they are caught in something of a bind. Despite what is often perceived to be the case, the income of priests is fairly small and declining and Mass stipends are an important supplementary income, which they cannot really afford to turn their backs on. So we have allowed the practice to develop and even encouraged it, by announcing at the beginning of the Mass who it is being said for, while knowing well that this makes no theological sense. If we could find some other way of assuring the priest of proper financial support, then we might begin to make headway in getting rid of stipends altogether.

In our generation the Mass has become completely overused. With the collapse of the old devotions after the Vatican Council, the Mass tended to be put on for every occasion. It was the easy way out – a lazy response to the problem of the time. What was needed were new forms of liturgy, more appropriate to the age, to replace the old devotion. But that would have taken considerable work and imagination. It was simpler and less challenging to say Mass. And our laziness could always be covered up by a little speech on the significance of the Mass, how it was the great Christian prayer. That is true but it is not the only Christian prayer and its overuse has meant that it has lost a lot of its power and significance. The laziness of the Irish Church has also been shown in the lack of variety and involvement in the celebration of Mass. Almost invariably the priest is up on the altar doing his thing. At most there may be a lay reader and a Eucharistic minister but the involvement of the talents of the community in the form of paraliturgies is hardly ever considered. In this we are way behind other countries. Some of the parishes in Britain and North America have far greater life and vitality than the average Irish one.

I attended the Easter vigil in a church in South Carolina recently. It was a most impressive celebration, with a great number of people involved, and all playing their parts in a most professional manner. Nothing was rushed or slipshod. It began at 7.30 p.m. and I asked the person who dropped me to the church and who did not wish to attend himself, to call back for me at 9.00 p.m., presuming that it would be over by then. But by nine we had not yet got to the offertory! And still nobody was restless or in any hurry. It was a real community celebration of the resurrection and I got a sense that they regarded it as the most important thing they would do over the Easter; they had no problem giving it time.

In most of the surveys done on the Mass, it is the homily or sermon that tends to come in for the main criticism. It is usually described as boring, uninteresting, too long and lacking in real content. For me, who does the bulk of my preaching in the context of special events, like missions and novenas, I think it is fair to say that preaching at a Sunday Mass is much more difficult. People come to special events with a different mindset. They are there to hear what you have to say, and they are open to listening. At Sunday Mass, for whatever reason, people are much less geared towards listening and giving time. From the moment they enter the door of the church they seem to want to get it over with and get out again. I am sure there are many reasons for this. One of the main ones has to do with the fact that Sunday Mass was seen for so long as an obligation, something that had to be done, whereas when people come to a special event they come of their own free will. It is part of the price we have to pay for the generations who were told that if they did not attend Mass every Sunday they would be committing a mortal sin for each occasion that they missed. This was part of the control mentality of the Church. If you impose a sufficiently fearful sanction, then you will force people to behave in a certain way. They will not do so with the freedom and openness, however, needed to bring real life to the event. I have a lot of sympathy for the priest whose only experience of preaching is at the Sunday Mass. It must be hard to work up energy week after week when faced with what can seem like an impenetrable wall of apathy.

It is also true that the type of preparation for preaching that young priests undergo in most seminaries is totally inadequate. Many come out without even the most basic principles on voice projection or use of a microphone. The biggest problem of all is the lack of apprenticeship. There is a strong culture among diocesan priests that they do not comment on each other's sermons, beyond making some polite and fairly meaningless remark. In most cases a young priest is put out into a parish and no other priest, or person with expertise in communication, ever gives him a critique of his preaching or any help on how to improve. And he will hear little or nothing from the people. I have known of many cases where the poor quality of a priest's preaching was common talk among the people, but no one said anything to himself about it. The real failure is within the clerical structure itself. Each young priest should have a period of a few years during which his preaching is regularly monitored and critiqued, and professional help given where needed. I wonder, since the life of a priest involves so much public performance, whether there is an argument to be made that skill in public communication should be a prerequisite for ordination, particularly today, when people expect very high standards in this area? Another solution would be for the priest to delegate the task of preaching to members of the community who have more talent in this area. I know that Canon Law forbids this. It says that only an ordained minister can preach the homily at the Eucharist. But if Canon Law is an obstacle to the real celebration of the Eucharist, and I believe it is in this case, then surely the idea should be considered. In the scale of Christian values the Eucharist is infinitely more important than Canon Law.

I remember once visiting a parish where the priest, a young man, was very shy and had a soft, timid voice. By itself, without any amplification, his voice would not carry beyond the front seat. He informed me when I arrived that the sound system wasn't working, and when I asked him what had happened I discovered that even though it had not been functioning for a few weeks, he had done nothing about it. A quick phone call produced an electrician who replaced a fuse and we were on the air again. I wondered why this man had gone weeks without amplification and had not got it repaired. As I got to know him during the week, I discovered the depths of his shyness and came to the conclusion that he was perfectly happy not to have any microphone, because he found it much easier to cope when he knew that the people did not hear him. This man needed a lot of professional help but was not getting any, because no one, either clerical or lay, was attending to him. It would surely have made more sense for someone else to perform the task of preaching in that parish, and leave the priest, who was a kind and gentle man, to perform his ministry is ways more suited to his personality.

Preaching, like any form of public speaking, is an art. Some people are naturally good at it and others, no matter how hard they work, just haven't got the talent and remain dull and uninteresting. I can remember one man I worked with who used to put enormous energy into preparing his sermons. He wrote and rewrote them many times. He read and studied endlessly, his head was full with all the background information that he could possibly need. He came to the pulpit with the final product all typed out and perfectly honed. Unfortunately the more he worked, the worse the sermon got. He had a very flat, boring voice and spoke in a monotone. Even the most learned and original ideas dropped dead as they came out of his mouth. He never made a preacher and it was sad for him because he worked so hard at it. It is not generally true, however, that hard work is so futile. Most people, if they work hard at their sermons, do improve.

In contrast to him, I remember sitting in a hall full of young people while a priest stood on the stage giving them a talk. This man took the microphone in his hand and sauntered out to the front of the stage. He had no notes of any type with him but he spoke freely and easily. He was tall, good-looking and radiated personality. I was the only older person in the hall and I was fascinated with what was happening. Because of my age the speaker did not have the same power over me that he had over the young people. I was not swept away by his appearance and personality. I could see clearly that he had prepared nothing and that he was waffling off the top of his head. He was so confident in his ability to communicate that he had got lazy and didn't bother to prepare anything anymore. He spoke for over half an hour and never for a moment lost the riveted attention of the audience. What he was communicating had little or nothing to do with what he was saying and equally little to do with the Christian message but it was very powerful communication. When the mission was over and we were leaving the parish one of us overheard a group of teenage girls discussing this man and saying how heartbroken they were that he was leaving: 'Oh, why did he come here at all, breaking our hearts!'

On another occasion I was working on a mission, where we had two separate arrangements, one for the youth and one for adults. On this particular night I was not speaking at either, so I went from one to the other. The youth event was being addressed by one of our students. He was a young man who was very unsure of himself, and his posture proclaimed that loudly. He could not stand upright, hunched his shoulders and constantly swayed from side to side, shuffling his feet. He fiddled and fidgeted with the microphone, and looked at the ground rather than at the audience. Yet he spoke in a very personal manner. His obvious vulnerability and lack of confidence drew a sympathetic response from the young people, who could see themselves in him. And his openness and honesty were powerful. In the course of fifteen minutes he violated all the rules of good public speaking but he gave a magnificent talk and never lost attention for one moment. Everyone in the church felt like going up and putting their arms around him. In contrast the priest speaking at the adult mission had marvellous style. He was tall, erect, and had a beautifully modulated voice. He made great use of dramatic pauses and talked very directly to the people. But he had a tendency to rely too much on his acquired skills and on this particular night he had nothing prepared. Though he spoke for half an hour the content of his talk left a lot to be desired. At no stage did he say anything remotely personal. It was one of those talks that sound good while you are listening to it, and then when it is over you wonder what it was about. Later on that night, when I returned to my monastery, I reported that I had heard two sermons, one full of content with no style, the other one all style and no content!

One of the great curses of preaching is the 'preaching tone'. By that I mean the type of artificial sounding voice that some priests put on when they begin to preach. I am not sure where this comes from but it is the death knell of good preaching. I remember one man who was in ordinary life a brilliant storyteller. He could entertain people sitting around a fire with one funny story after another, marvellously told. He had a keen gift of observation and great colourful descriptions of the characters he met on his work. He was the best of good company. But when he mounted the pulpit he changed totally. His voice became heavy and solemn – 'preachy'. Once, in later life, I heard him trying to tell one of his funny stories during a sermon and it fell totally flat, because his voice and the language he was using were too artificial. At some stage, either during his training or in his early years as a priest, he had taken on this artificial tone and nobody had ever helped him to get out of it. He obviously believed that this was the proper way to preach. It was a shame, because with his marvellous gifts of storytelling he could have been a great preacher.

In today's world of advanced communication techniques the straight talk is now a fairly primitive method of getting a message across. It still has, and presumably always will have its place, and when it is well done it can be very powerful. But we should not depend on it to the exclusion of everything else. There are many other ways of communicating a message at a Sunday Mass and we should vary our presentation much more than we do. Each community has people with a variety of skills that could be used, in terms of drama, mime, dance, music, song and many others. If a priest could involve people like this and be imaginative in the way he presents the message each Sunday, be willing to push out the boundaries of Church law in this area, then the possibilities are endless. It is certainly time that we listened to the consistent complaints of people that they experience the Mass as boring and uninteresting. Our usual answer that Mass is not meant to be entertaining is not adequate. It is certainly meant to engage the minds and hearts of people and if it does that they will not be bored. I know it involves faith on their part too.

We can presume now, since the idea of attending Mass out of fear of committing mortal sin is dying out rapidly, that most of the people who are present have at least some little amount of faith or they would not be there in the first place. We need to take their criticisms seriously and begin to act on them. It is my experience that there is still a great number of lay people, young and old, who have a strong faith and who are willing and anxious to be involved at all levels in the Church and the celebration of the liturgy. In fact it is among them that I find the real vitality of the Irish Church today. The clerical church is by and large old and somewhat demoralised, lacking the verve and energy needed to try new things, whereas the lay people are going off studying theology, liturgy, liturgical music, creative drama and lots of other areas that would bring our Masses back to life. If we do not use them and give them scope in the next few years, many of them will become disillusioned and drift away. If that happens I doubt if their equivalent will be available to the Church in the next generation.

Numbers are undoubtedly declining at our weekend Masses – I will return to that issue in the final chapter – but here I would like to make a few suggestion as to how we tackle the problem of bringing the Mass back to life for the people. We have far too many Masses for the number of people who are attending, and as a consequence the congregations are much too dispersed. It is difficult to do much with a Mass if there is just a small group of people lost in a large church. We need to reduce the number of Masses substantially and then we will also have more energy to concentrate on improving the quality of the remainder. For this to happen the often intense competition that takes place between churches and parishes needs to be eliminated. And of course this is bound up with money. More people at Mass means a bigger income for the parish and for the priest. So that is another reason why the system of funding priests needs to be looked at.

We need to make a much greater effort to involve the people who are attending, by establishing various liturgy groups in the parish and inviting them to become members. These groups would cover all the range of ministries involved in the Mass, singing, reading, preparing and presenting the homily, distributing the Eucharist, creating the proper atmosphere and ambience in the church for prayer and celebration. The ultimate aim in this would be to create a situation where every believer in the parish would see the Sunday Eucharist as the celebration of the whole community and be sure that they were all working together in partnership to make it the best possible celebration. Good singers are needed and themselves need to be trained how to lead and encourage a congregation in participation. Most communities would have a number of people with the potential to do this, given proper training, encouragement and support. A fully trained, professional liturgist, preferably a lay person, of whom there is an increasing number, could be hired by each deanery, or number of parishes, to work with all the different groups and provide the fresh ideas and initiatives necessary to maintain enthusiasm. It is not easy to decide whether it is better to depend on the voluntary talent of the local community or to hire someone trained professionally to cater for the different aspects of good liturgy. A strong argument can be made for drawing on the local talent, which in very many cases will be offered freely and generously. The difficulty with people who volunteer to do a service is that they can become very possessive of their role and very difficult to remove, and consequently can be a major barrier to development. There is a strong tendency in human nature to try to possess your own bit of turf, and in that context it is easier to deal with someone who is contracted and being paid for their work.

However these issues may be dealt with, I believe it true that the role of leader of the community in the Eucharist is the most important function of the priest in the parish and that the major part of his energy and effort should go into doing this as well as he possibly can. I also suspect that the future of the faith in this country will stand or fall to a fair degree on how well this task is performed.

8

Missed Opportunities
Unasked Questions

The Church – and the religious congregation to which I belong – are very different now from what they were when I made my life commitment all those years ago. I have lived through a time of enormous decline in both. A lot of the life has gone out of them. The vitality and excitement that inspired me during those years immediately before my ordination have been largely dissipated, as the personnel have grown older and as the Church turned away from the spirit that imbued the Vatican Council in the sixties. The great sense of hope for the future that we had then has mostly proved to be illusory. The life of a priest in the Catholic Church in Ireland in the last quarter-century has turned out to be very different to what I expected it to be. As my life has gone on I have had to find energy and enthusiasm from sources other than the two great institutions to which I committed my life.

In the early seventies there was a fairly strong sense of security in the Irish Church. Although there were some indications that things were changing and there were signs of trouble ahead it was still common to have full churches on a

Sunday morning. Despite some decline in numbers entering seminaries and convents, there were a good few vocations and nobody really expected the almost total collapse of vocations that we are experiencing today. In fact there was a lot of complacency in our attitude in those years. In order to see into the future, all we had to do was look elsewhere: at the Continent, where we could see the almost empty churches; and at North America, where the beginnings of the child-abuse trouble was emerging. I think there was a strong though mostly unstated belief that the Irish Catholic Church was different, that these sorts of things happened elsewhere but that they would not happen in Ireland.

We had a strong pride in our Church. Hadn't our ancestors died for the faith and would we in our time desert it? It is hard to understand where this mentality came from, this notion that we in Ireland were special, that we were the island of saints and scholars and that what happened in 'pagan' places like America and the Continent would not happen among us. I think this pride was a significant factor that created a great deal of complacency and contributed to our unwillingness to face what was really happening at that time. A lot was taking place that should have given us ample warning of what was to come. Two things stand out for me: the drop in the number of vocations and of those attending Sunday Mass. An example of the first concerns a convent I knew. It enjoyed the usual influx of vocations through the fifties and sixties up to 1964. Yet anyone who joined that particular convent from 1965 until the end of the decade had left by the mid-seventies. Some really significant change in attitude had taken place at that time. I witnessed the same type of exodus in the seminary I myself attended.

However, instead of forcing us really to examine the system, these departures were usually dismissed in one sentence: 'They never really had a vocation.' The talismanic notion of 'vocation' enabled us to avoid facing the reality that the system was no longer a healthy organism.

The phenomenon of a sizeable number of people not going to Mass was observable among two significant groups: third-level students and the urban working class. While some of these may have returned to the Church and sacraments in later years, particularly when their children were growing up, the social norm of Sunday Mass attendance had been dislodged and would never again have the same power to control behaviour. I remember that one night during my seminary years a few of us were sitting around discussing the state of the Church and someone said that our churches would be empty in twenty years. He was, maybe, a little pessimistic in his prophecy but we can see that he was closer to the truth than those of us who believed that things would continue to go on largely as they had been. Many of us couldn't risk saying what he said, because if we did we would have had to face our own personal painful choices. It was easier to be in denial and that was the prevalent attitude in the Church until quite recently: a belief that somehow we were going to ride out the storm. A great many priests tended to put their heads down and continue as they always had done, unaware that they were becoming anachronisms in their own time. Now things have gone so far that priests are being forced to recognise the situation, and the effect on their morale is often disastrous. When I look back on the late sixties and early seventies in the Irish Church, I think of it mostly as a period of missed opportunities, of unasked questions. What were the questions we should have asked? I think they fall generally into the following categories.

First, we failed to question the role of the Papacy.

Back in the Autumn of 1978 I was working on a mission in the parish of Corofin in County Clare. There is a little church in that parish called Rath. It is a lovely place and on a fine evening I was walking in the gate leading to the church for the evening mission service. Some of the local men were standing at the gate and they said to me: 'Did you hear the news?'

'No' I said, 'what news?'

'We have a new Pope,' they told me, 'and he is from Poland.'

I was delighted. We had broken away from the old Italian hegemony. It seemed to be very much in tune with the whole spirit of change of the time. He was a relatively young man, from eastern Europe, a playwright, in touch with life, and gave promise of a fresh new beginning. The following year he came to Ireland. Looking back on that now it was an amazing event. The whole country came to a standstill and massive crowds went to see him in the different places where he spoke. I was at the youth event in Galway. In hindsight that occasion is laden with irony, in that the two big performers, apart from the Pope, were Eamonn Casey and Michael Cleary. But it was by any standards a remarkable event. Young people had gathered from all over the country, and, as young people do, there were out to enjoy themselves. They cheered and clapped for everything and everyone. The Pope, performer that he is, responded to them and rose to the occasion. In my mind the event will always be associated with going to see John F. Kennedy in Galway sixteen years earlier, when he addressed us all in Eyre Square and talked in poetic language about looking out over Galway Bay to his home in Boston.

I was younger then and more impressionable. By 1979 I had become less easy to impress and I thought that the conclusions drawn from the Pope's visit by the Church in Ireland were both foolish and damaging. They served to deepen the already existing complacency at a time when massive challenges were facing us and needed to be met. The official Church, seeing the great crowds and the enthusiasm, concluded that the people still had the faith and that there was no need to worry. Some even concluded that the event in Galway was a sign that the young people, too, were strong in their faith and loyalty to the Church. For people like me who worked with them day in and day out, that was blatant nonsense. The young people reacted that day as they would to a pop star and it meant little more than that. And the effect of the Pope's last speech, his one in Limerick where he gave out his usual traditional line on family values, was to resurrect the contraception issue, which I, in my role as a confessor, did not appreciate.

As I write this the Pope has just returned from a visit to Cuba. He is now an old man, feeble and tired-looking. But he is still driven by a powerful will and determination and, I have no doubt, great faith. He has been in many ways a great and charismatic leader and he will be given credit historically for the collapse of the communist regimes in eastern Europe. I have never been, and as time goes on I am even less, an admirer of him. He has been far too autocratic and dictatorial in his style of leadership, and one of the serious effects of his long reign has been deeply to divide the Church. He has allowed himself to be greatly influenced, and to be seen to be so, by some extremely traditionalist groups who have become massively powerful during his pontificate. For a leader to identify himself too much with a position that is on the extreme of the Church is not good leadership. His treatment of alternative points of view and the silencing of theologians, particularly in the earlier years of his reign, was scandalous. Maybe most damaging of all has been his policy of appointing bishops and cardinals. He has done his best to fill all the leadership positions in the Church with people who think like himself. That is not the way to promote unity and harmony in an organisation. His style of leadership has been such that in certain circles a person's Catholicism is judged not by his faith in Jesus Christ but by his loyalty to the Pope. In that way he has, unfortunately, become a sign of division rather than of unity.

I know that there are some people within the Church who will be appalled at a priest writing in this way about the Pope. For them loyalty to the Holy Father is a central tenet of the faith. I have never felt like that. I believe that even a cursory look at the history of the Papacy will confirm my view. Down through the years there have been Popes who were good men and bad men, Popes who were saintly and others who were corrupt, Popes who were good leaders and did great things for the Church, and others who were very bad leaders and did great damage. I suppose it is part of our reaction to the Protestant Reformation and the rejection of the Pope that we in the Catholic Church, and especially in Ireland, have tended to elevate him beyond human level to a sort of semi-divine status.

There has also been a general failure to question the

structure of government in the Church and perhaps the diocesan system in particular. A story, probably apocryphal, is told about a junior assistant pastor in a large Catholic parish in Chicago. News came of the Pope's death and he, oppressed by all the layers of bureaucracy above him, greeted the news with this question: 'Does that mean we all get to move up a step?' And that, in a way, sums up how it works. It is a system of steps, each of which is taken in order of seniority and at the prescribed time. If the Church was an ordinary commercial enterprise, it would have gone to the wall a long time ago. It works on a very rigid system that does not take kindly to any type of deviation from the norm and instead of making an effort to put people of talent into positions that would suit them, the system is normally followed to the letter, irrespective of the consequences.

I presume that most people at this stage are well acquainted with the method by which bishops are appointed. Fr Joe Dunn outlined that very well in his book *No Lions in the Hierarchy*. In the last twenty years it has been generally accepted, and it would also be my experience that, with a few exceptions, men were chosen not because of their leadership qualities, but because of their orthodoxy. There has been a preference in many cases to appoint quiet, academic characters, with little or no pastoral experience. There are many examples of people of great talent and leadership ability who have been passed over, because they were not perceived to be orthodox, particularly in relation to contraception, celibacy and the ordination of women. These three issues have tended to be the litmus test of orthodoxy in this generation. I suspect that a significant degree of damage has been done to the Church by allowing these factors to be so influential in the choosing of people for leadership positions. The irony of it all is that the power of a bishop is quite limited. To be in a position of supposed leadership, where you have to constantly look to Rome to make sure you are not in any way deviating from the official position, is very unsatisfactory. I often think that the job, rather than being one of real leadership, is more in the category of civil servant, implementing the decisions handed down from above. Not only have you to be careful not to displease the Roman authorities but you have the media watching your every utterance to see is there is even the slightest sign of rebellion, which they could turn into a banner headline, which would be duly noted by the Vatican and carefully filed away. No wonder many of our bishops seem to be such safe and colourless characters. It is true for Joe Dunn. There are no lions in the hierarchy.

We joke about how a man will never have a hungry day – or be told the truth – after he becomes a bishop but we have not seriously questioned the type of almost sycophantic subservience that often exists between a bishop and his priests. This is changing but much more slowly that one might expect. Some bishops act and are treated by their priests almost like feudal lords, sitting at the head of the table and dominating the conversation, with nobody daring to contradict them or present an alternative point of view. Behind all this they are often lonely, isolated people. The saddest part for me of John Bowman's two excellent programmes on John Charles McQuaid on RTÉ television in the early summer of 1998 was the account of the woman acquaintance of his who told how, once he was made to resign in 1972, he no longer had any friends. Those who had appeared to be close to him while he was still in office quickly disappeared and he was a lonely man in the end. I know this is what can happen with those in positions of power. They gather around them people who are self-serving and opportunistic, trying to climb on the back of the person in power to advance their own careers. It is sad to see that it happens also in the Church, an organisation that is purporting to stand for an entirely different set of values.

The one area where bishops have some real power is that of appointing priests to parishes and it has proved very hard to break the pattern of appointing them according to seniority rather than suitability. Often their best years are well behind them before they are made parish priests. In many dioceses there are young energetic men in positions of subservience, where they have little scope for their energy and enthusiasm, while men who are long past the normal retiring age are holding down the major posts. Change is coming now but it is coming because of the decline in the number of priests, rather than a recognition of the need for change. So it is the old story. The Church reverses into change rather than initiating it.

Part of the problem with the diocesan system is that we have not sufficiently questioned the role of the priest. In my years as a mission preacher I have come to know a great many of the priests around this country. The majority of them are admirable men, committed and caring, and living very unselfish lives. Yet we as a body have presided over a period of serious decline in the life of the Church. History will probably record our failure and be very critical of us. Why has this been so? I think that as a group we are very institutionalised. We have bought into the clerical caste system and have failed to look outside it for the answers to the problems that presented themselves. Our thinking has been much too narrow and hidebound by the system. I have always been conscious of how much on the defensive priests are, how easily our hackles rise at the slightest hint of criticism, even when it is well-disposed and coming from committed people. We are not good at listening when it comes to an evaluation of our role, and that has prevented us from both learning and developing.

It is significant that the involvement of laity has made much less progress in Ireland than in equivalent Catholic Churches in the western world. We, the clergy, have clung too much to our own position of status and power. We have not been willing to share with the lay people, and in my experience the main source of vitality in the Irish Church today is with the laity. On a mission I am much more likely to find fresh ideas and the enthusiasm to implement them from the laity than from the clergy. I've had recent experience of working in parishes in Sligo and in Athenry. In both cases some members of the local theatre group expressed their willingness to be involved in the mission in whatever way my fellow missioner and I could facilitate them. They were exceptionally talented in both speaking and acting. So, during the week we tried a number of different ways, through drama, mime, music, to present some aspects of the Gospel message. It was an exhilarating experience for us. It opened up all sorts of new possibilities for preaching and liturgy. It confirmed me in my belief that the traditional homily or sermon is no longer an adequate instrument to carry the whole burden of communication in church. But mostly it showed what an exciting future there could be if we really developed a partnership between all members of the Church, working together to the same end. The traditional Church that we have known, the one dominated by a clerical male elite, would appear to be coming to the end of its time. Clergy are showing all the signs of tiredness and lack of energy. Yet we cling to what we have and will let go only when we have to. So many of our attitudes, unfortunately, have to do with power, and all the indications are that there will have to be much more substantial decline in the clerical church before any new life can get a real chance to flourish.

I am aware that not all the blame rests with the priests in this area. Shakespeare puts it this way:

The fault . . . is not in our stars,
But in ourselves, that we are underlings.

In places where priests have tried to hand over the reins of power and decision-making to their parishioners, two interrelated factors have hindered their efforts. Firstly, many lay people want the *status quo* to continue. It suits them. They are conditioned to see the priest as the authority figure. There is a certain attraction for some people in having a person who will make the decisions for them. It takes the responsibility from their own shoulders. Secondly, people can accept the decisions of the priest more easily than they can those of a mere fellow parishioner. They see the priest as somebody apart, rather than as a parishioner like themselves. He can be regarded as a neutral, diplomatic figure who can better please all factions in the parish.

My own religious congregation, the Redemptorists, has experienced enormous decay and disintegration, particularly in the developed world, in the years since I became a member thirty-five years ago. Like most religious congregations here we are now an ageing group, with an average age of well over sixty and only a handful of younger men. Even though I have lived through the half-century I am still one of the younger members of the community where I live. Conversation at daily meals tends to be more about the latest sickness of one of the brothers than about the state of the Church or how we might do our work more effectively. The vitality has departed with our youth. There was a time when we had a degree of radicalism in our thinking and our work, and I have highlighted in this book some areas where I feel we made a contribution to the life of the Church, especially in our efforts to adapt the practice of confession, in the stand we took on the contraception issue and probably also in the impact of the large novenas to Our Lady. Now, looking back, I can see that our radicalism wasn't anything like as radical as we thought it was at the time. We have always been too clerical, too comfortably at home in (and a part of) the system to be really radical, and so much of our energy has gone into upholding and bolstering forms of the institutional Church that I do not see now as helpful.

But whatever about that, we had energy in those days. Now, as befits our age structure, we are more anxious to conserve the familiar and the tried and trusted. For a long period I had great enthusiasm for the life of the congregation, playing my part on councils and committees both at national and international level, and I did my stint as a superior. I enjoyed the cut and thrust of debate and argued vehemently for change during the amazing and often disturbing times we lived through. I find it harder and harder now to find the energy for that side of my life. Overseeing the death throes of a once thriving institution is not very pleasant, and more and more of my age group in all religious orders are tending to opt out of positions of responsibility and to, in a sense, do our own thing. It may not be a good development but I think it is a necessary one if the individual is to survive. Probably because of all of this turmoil there is something of a crisis in the individual lives of many of us, which each of us in our own way has been struggling with in recent years. When you see little future for the institution to which you have committed your life, when you no longer have energy or enthusiasm for it, it is not easy to stay on and to retain one's sanity.

It is interesting to observe how an institution tries to cope with the type of collapse that we have experienced. A great deal of denial goes on. One of the ways denial works is to set up more and more structures. We in our congregation now have a far more time-consuming and complex system of government than ever before, at a time when our ability to control our destiny is at its weakest. I see the same pattern in other religious institutions. We spend an inordinate amount of time electing our government every three years, while there are fewer and fewer people available to implement any of the decisions reached.

The one question that has been asked, especially in recent years, is how a Church which exercised substantial control over the sexual lives of people could be guilty of so much mismanagement in that area when it came to its own priests. The last ten years or so have been most of all the period of the scandals in the Church. We have lived through the drama of Bishop Eamonn Casey's relationship with Annie Murphy and his escape into exile, the allegations about Michael

Cleary and many other priests, and, worst of all, the revelations about the priests, brothers and sisters who have been involved in child abuse, physical and sexual. The revelations about Bishop Casey neither surprised nor shocked me. I suppose I had come to know too much both about human nature in general, and about priests in particular, to be easily shocked.

I did not know Eamonn Casey well. But during his time as bishop we Redemptorists launched an annual novena in Galway cathedral. It was an immediate success, and still thrives. The response the first few years was amazing, both in terms of numbers and the enthusiasm of the people. I was very involved and consequently had some dealings with the bishop. The conduct of the novena was largely our affair and we decided how it would be done. But where it impinged in any way on the ordinary life of the cathedral or the diocese, issues would naturally have to be discussed with the local authorities. I can recall a number of occasions during those early years when we raised some of these issues or made suggestions. Suffice to say that in my experience Bishop Casey was not a ready listener. On the contrary, I found him to be an old-style authoritarian whose tendency was to lay down the law without feeling the need to listen to anyone. This was in sharp contrast to his public image. But, sadly, public image tends to be what endures in this TV age.

I was shocked, like most people, by all that we have learned of the sexual abuse of children by priests and religious, and even more so by the attempts by the Church authorities in the early stages to cover things up, although it must be said that they did eventually take control and are now generally acting very responsibly. While the sexual abuse of a child by a priest or religious, or indeed by any adult, is somewhat inexplicable, even revolting, yet, as I have said elsewhere, attempts to portray abusers as beasts and demons do not really fit the reality as I have known it. I have known, and even for periods of time lived with, some of the priests who have been convicted of abuse, and in many ways they were good, kind and caring individuals. That is the complex reality of child abuse that we as a society have yet to come to grips with. If it were beasts and demons who did these things it would be much easier to deal with. Instead they seem to be people who are perfectly ordinary, and even good, in other aspects of their lives: the family member, the relation, the friend, the person next door, even the local priest or teacher.

We all experienced the outbreak of anger against the Church as the scandals began to unfold. I, like many other priests, both shared the anger and felt the brunt of it. It was a strange sensation to be revolted by something and at the same time to feel tainted by it due to the fact that it had been committed by someone from our own profession. I'm sure swimming coaches, teachers and others are feeling the same now as the problem increasingly affects more and more of the professions. While some of the media coverage was unfair and sensationalist, I believe that the anger felt by people was perfectly understandable. It had to do with all the power that the Church had exercised over people's lives for so long, especially over their sexual lives. A letter I got recently from a married woman and mother of a grown family illustrates what I am saying here. (I will alter the details to protect the anonymity of the people involved).

In the sixties, when I was in my early twenties, and new to this town, myself and my friend went to Dublin to a concert with two young men our own age. Since the concert was going to be late, we booked into a hotel in Dublin for the night. The following week the local priest in this town called to the office where I worked and asked to speak to me. He demanded to know what had happened when we got to the hotel, who had slept with whom. I was mortified; in those days we were so innocent. He assumed that I had shared a room with one of the boys. 'Now,' he said, 'tell me the truth, as I have already spoken to the other three.' Then he informed me that he would speak to my parents about the situation. As I was interviewed in front of all my colleagues, I was totally embarrassed. My other three friends said that if he spoke to our parents they would never again go to Mass and sadly they haven't done so. Luckily it did not put me off the practice of my faith. The priest died recently. I am sorry now that I never confronted him.

Thirty-four years later, and a committed Catholic, this woman is obviously still angry over the incident. And her anger is directed at that priest not just because he set himself up as a moral policeman but also that he used bullying tactics towards her. She is sorry she did not confront him. There will clearly be a lot of confronting going on in the next few years!

A good bit of the anger has to do with the rigid enforcement of the law on contraception which I have dealt with elsewhere. People were naturally angry when they discovered that a priest like Michael Cleary, who had been a vehement proponent of the official line on contraception and on Catholic Church teaching on sexuality generally may not have been practising in his own life what he preached. Michael Cleary had written a column in one of our national papers for a few years and I was constantly irritated by the way he insistently churned out a hard, unbending line on all moral issues and seemed to make no effort to reach out to people who were struggling in their own lives. I have been told that he could be very understanding in dealing with individuals but in his writings he was always rigid and unbending, seeming to be very careful not to be seen to be in any way out of line.

If it is true that he himself was struggling in the area of sexuality, his attitude, as portrayed in his writings, is more baffling still. Or maybe it isn't. He may have had some type of split personality in relation to his sexuality, and his writings could be interpreted as one part of his psyche attempting to deny, and even condemn, what was happening in this other part of his life. Human nature, as we are increasingly learning, is very complex. But it wouldn't be right to lay all the blame at Michael Cleary's door. He was in a sense being used by the Church. As its certainties weakened, as church attendance declined, many priests and lay people put Michael Cleary on a pedestal and found security in his larger-than-life personality. He simplified issues for them. He was the epitome of 'the grand man'. He could fill a church, defend the Pope, preach traditional Catholicism, lull people into the belief that the faith was still strong among the plain people of Ireland and that we would all be fine were it not for a handful of intellectuals, malcontents and media gurus. On top of all that he was entertaining and nobody said that *his* Mass was boring. It doesn't give me any pleasure to write like this about a man who is dead but already I can see the tendency to do the same with other people in the Church, to create an unreal image of them so that they can perform the same function that he had. It is time we learned the lesson that all people have feet of clay, and that as Christians we must find our security in Christ rather than in any human person.

Abuse of people comes in many forms, and physical or sexual abuse were not the only ways in which the Church misused its power over people in the past. Indeed, I strongly suspect that some forms of what I would call 'spiritual abuse' may have done greater damage, since this type of abuse was much more widespread. I recently came across what I consider to be a very good explanation of this in an article written for a parish bulletin in the US by Fr Clement D. Thibodeau. It is presented as part of an apology for all the abuse committed by Church people in the past:

> Some priests, and other Church professionals, have abused people spiritually, claiming to have power to exclude people from the Church and its sacraments. Some priests have told people they were excommunicated when it was not so. Some priests have turned people away when they came to get married. Some priests have denied absolution in confession when they should not have done so. (Church law does tie our hands at times: but sometimes it is just personal interpretation by the priest!) Spiritual abuse will be

punished by God more severely than sexual abuse. It is of the heart and soul rather than of the body.

Priests are not trusted today. I see it all the time. Youth have been told to hold their distance. Men think that priests are all homosexuals. They shy away from us. Women are not sure whether we will exploit them and hurt them. I find it most painful.

I know that many priests, and some who certainly did not deserve it, were very hurt by things that were said to them around the time of these scandals but there was a funny side to it too. One day I was driving from Galway to Limerick, dressed casually. There were two young female students hitching a lift outside Gort. Guessing that they were returning to university in Limerick I brought them along. They were very friendly and full of talk. On the way we got around to discussing the dangers of hitching and I was highly amused when one of them said: 'I wouldn't mind who I got a lift from, as long as it wasn't from a priest!' I waited until we got to the point where I was leaving them off and then I could not resist telling her that her worst fears had been actualised. We all had a good laugh over it.

A big question for everyone in recent years, but one not sufficiently faced up to yet in the Catholic Church, has been the nature of commitment. When I was ordained, even though I did not myself fully share the conviction and some people we knew had already begun to leave the priesthood, there was still a general acceptance by the priests themselves, which was reinforced by public expectation, that we were in this for life and that unless something really exceptional happened, we would continue as priests until we died. This seems to be no longer the case with many of the young generation of priests. I first noticed this about twelve years ago when a newly ordained young man said to me, 'I will give it ten years and see how it is going.'

To enter the priesthood with that mentality was a whole new reality, but I suppose he was doing no more than expressing the way of thinking of his generation. He had grown up with change and with the sense that nothing is permanent any longer. The notion of staying with one profession for life is now foreign to much of modern thinking and is affecting all walks of life, including marriage. I don't know how the priesthood is going to come to terms with this.

A further indication of a trend towards short-term commitment is the process by which some men leave the priesthood now. It used to be considered an enormous thing to do, with a certain disgrace and opprobrium attached to it. There tended to be a lot of complications with family members and great efforts were made to keep it secret. If it happened that the priest was on the foreign missions when he left, the preference often was that he would stay there and not return, and in that way his departure might be kept quiet. Once a person began to think seriously in terms of leaving he immediately ceased to perform as a priest until such time as he had made up his mind. But now things seem to have changed immensely both in terms of the person leaving and of the people's perception of him. Recently I observed the sequence of a man's departure after about seven or eight years as a priest. I know that he went through a long and careful process of making his decision, using what professional help was available along the way. But when he finally made his decision to leave, the procedure was very different to what it would have been a generation ago. He first began to apply for, and eventually succeeded in getting, a job for himself. Then he fixed the date of his departure. Having sorted out his life in this way, he continued to work on as a priest until the week before he was due to take up his new job. The fact that he was leaving did not prevent him from continuing to say Mass, hear confession and do all the public duties of a priest right up to the day of his departure. This would have been utterly unheard of in the old days. In this sense, leaving the priesthood is being seen more and more as a matter of changing from one profession to another, rather than a cataclysmic event in a person's life, which brought disgrace not only on himself, but also on his family. If I am correct in my observations, the two developments I have cited here will have major effect on the priesthood as we have known it.

The Church has attempted to stifle questioning and discussion about the ordination of women. In adopting this attitude it has appeared to me foolish, even pathetic. This century has seen enormous developments in the whole range of issues related to women and their place in society. It is clear that the time has come for all aspects of this topic to be explored. For the Vatican to attempt to stifle discussion is useless. Even an institution as powerful as it perceives itself to be cannot turn back the tide of history. The attitude of the Church to women is fouled up by layers of fear and prejudice, coming from many different historical and theological sources, mostly from traditional Catholic teaching on sexuality, and also from the fact that its teaching has been shaped significantly by male celibates. I fear greatly that we do not have the ability to face the question of the place of women in the Church with any degree of clarity and openness and that by clinging to totally outmoded attitudes we will eventually drive women away.

The final issue that has not been addressed is the balance between the quality and the quantity of candidates for the priesthood. One or two generations ago, before the advent of free secondary education and the economic surge of the sixties, the priesthood tended to be one of the favourite professions for young men. The diocesan seminaries, especially Maynooth, could pick and choose from among their many applicants, so they often got the cream of the available talent. That fact makes it more difficult to accept the failure of the Irish Church to deal more imaginatively and effectively with the decline of recent years. It wasn't for want of academic ability in the ranks of the priests. But of course academic distinction is no guarantee of good inter-personal or pastoral skills, of courage in the face of difficult challenges, and least of all of spirituality. Now things are different; I understand that the bulk of students who apply for the priesthood today are much more average in academic terms. The priesthood is no longer seen as an attractive profession, so the really bright students, those with the highest number of points, tend to be drawn towards one of the other professions. I think that this will ultimately be to the detriment of the Church, insofar as it may lead to a decline in the quality of theological thinking and in the presentation of the intellectual basis for the faith.

Though I am not directly involved in this area of Church life, I'm told that there is some indication that young people who are particularly insecure, for whatever reason, are wishing to become priests in higher numbers than before. I suppose they might see the structured life of the priest as providing the type of protection they crave for in a constantly changing world. I don't know if this has any connection with a very noticeable trend of young priests who are very traditional in their outlook, and who are much more inclined to be seen dressed in black than the generation that went before them. The other trend which is generally accepted to be true is that a higher proportion than the average of people with homosexual tendencies are entering seminaries. They have every right to do so, and my observations would suggest that they make just as good priests as people of a heterosexual orientation, but if the priesthood ends up with considerably more homosexuals than the average, maybe there will be just cause for concern.

All the above questions, or failures to question, are issues for the collective Church. I have to face my own questions. I am fifty-one years of age. What choices do I want to make about the rest of my life? It would be reassuring to say that I have a plan worked out but in truth I haven't, any more than the next person. I don't know what the future holds for me. At the rate things are changing it is impossible to predict what the next twenty years will bring (if I live to the Biblical figure of seventy). As I come to the end of this book I offer this thought that has helped me and will perhaps help others.

Many years ago I heard the American Carmelite priest William McNamara discuss the Second Vatican Council. He told us that he had been talking about the event to a friend who was not Roman Catholic. The friend had just one question he wanted to ask about the bishops who would be attending the council. How many of them would be mystics? Fr McNamara didn't know the answer. Neither do I. But that little example raises the whole question of what is the true purpose of the Church, indeed of religion generally. In so far as I can answer that question, I think it has something to do with enabling all of us to become mystics. What do I mean by the word 'mystic'? I define a mystic as someone who contemplates the whole of life in the light of the Divine, in the light of something beyond and greater than this world. I believe that we professional religious people have spent too much energy in building up institutions that control, in passing laws that fix boundaries and in creating appropriate sanctions in order that the boundaries will not be breached, and in this way offering a type of certainty that is ultimately illusory.

There really are only two certainties, birth and death. And in between a great deal of our lives is made up of struggle and a significant degree of failure. When I was going to national school in Attymon I learned that we had five principal mysteries in our religion. They were the unity and trinity of God and the incarnation, death and resurrection of Christ. That was the answer that we learned off in the old language of the penny catechism. Now I have honed it down to something much simpler than that. Shakespeare puts it this way in *Hamlet*:

There's a divinity that shapes our ends,
Rough-hew them how we will.

The basic belief that I cling to is that there is a spirit, a God of love, who looks after all of us. When Christ died on Good Friday, people didn't know he was going to rise again on Easter Sunday. Maybe he didn't know himself. If we have the courage to face our own failures, to persevere through each one of our own dark nights, we come to a new phase of our lives, which we hope will be a bit richer and a bit wiser than the one that went before it. So, beyond the belief that there is a God who is constantly renewing the world and doing it out of love, I don't have many more answers. I do accept a further paradox that I see at the heart of it all. I believe that God is in charge of everything but because of the incarnation of Christ I, like every other human person, take my place in the great task of creation that God is constantly engaged in. I have to play my part in renewing the world. I can't sit back and be passive. I cannot say that it is not my business. And that is what keeps me going, just as it has kept people going for centuries and millennia, trying to love a little and to do good and even in a small way to make the world a better place. I have to remember that all the answers are somewhere in the heart of God, who is love.

I take consolation in the prayer of St Teresa of Avila, a woman who contemplated these matters with great wisdom:

Let nothing disturb you; nothing alarm you.
All things pass away.
God remains unchanged.
Be patient and you will obtain everything.
For with God in your heart, nothing is lacking.
God meets every one of your needs.